THE CAR
PAST & PRESENT

THE CAR
PAST & PRESENT

TED SMART

This edition produced by Ted Smart for
the Book People Ltd,
Guardian House,
Borough Road,
Godalming, Surrey GU7 2AE

ISBN 1-85613-049-5

Manufactured in Spain

Producer : Ted Smart
Author : Ken Vose
Edited by : Rupert O. Matthews
Book Design : Sara Cooper
Photo Research : Ed Douglas/Annie Price
Production Assistant : Seni Glaister

All photographs in this book
appear courtesy of
The National Motor Museum,
Beaulieu, Hampshire, England

with the exception of

pp2/3, 13(6), 33(8), 37(6), 44(1), 45(3 & 6),
61(5), 65(4), 92, 93, 94/95, 99 and 151(6)
which appear courtesy of Ron Kimball.

pp45(8), 46(3), 85(6), 118/119 and 161(3)
which appear courtesy of Jeffrey R. Zwart.

It was my father who created the link between the Montagu family and motoring, a link which has come to mean so much to me and to Beaulieu. Indeed the National Motor Museum was begun as a tribute to this man who, as a motorist since 1898, was one of the pioneer motorists of Britain and as a Member of Parliament was the first Parliamentary champion of the motorist's cause.

When, in 1952, I opened Palace House and its gardens to the public I displayed a handful of early vehicles in the Front Hall of the House, and it was from this modest beginning that the Museum was to grow. This did not happen overnight. Additional vehicles and items were added to the displays and installed in various parts of Palace House. By 1958 it became clear that it would be necessary to rehouse the exhibits in a building designed for the purpose in the grounds, as Palace House was being taken over by cars and beginning to take on the oily smell of a garage.

In 1959 the collection was moved to new premises in the grounds, but even that proved inadequate and in the mid-1960s a long term plan was drawn up. This was intended to increase accomodation for the museum, improve tourist facilities and yet harmonise with the countryside and centuries old buildings of Beaulieu. Leading architects were called in and instructed to fit the new museum, restaurant and car parks into the landscape so that they would be virtually invisible from outside the estate. This has been done with astonishing success. At the same time a charitable trust was established to own the collection. In 1972 the collection was re-opened as the National Motor Museum.

In the National Motor Museum, I have been able to bring together many of the great classic cars of the past hundred years, including several of my own particular dream cars. Of course the exact definition of a dream car is hard to pin down, and I would not imagine that my own particular taste is that of everyone who reads this book. Indeed there are probably nearly as many dream cars as there are dreamers.

Some prefer to concentrate on what the Americans call "muscle cars", vehicles unashamedly devoted to speed and power. Such dreams are made of low, sleek bodies, roaring engines and full, throaty growls. Yet those who dream of the ultimate in speed are destined never to be satisfied. Every new Ferrari or Aston Martin pushes the previous model into the twilight of forgotten dreams. Once their power and pace are surpassed, the fast cars lose much of their glamour and importance.

Others dream of cars of elegance and luxury. Here the famous marques are those of Rolls-Royce, Cadillac and Bugatti. These cars offer everything that could be wished for in the way of opulence and creature comforts. The plushly upholstered seats are contained within vehicles which give a ride so smooth and serene that one could be forgiven for thinking that an air cushion supported the car, rather than wheels and mechanics. But perhaps the great dream cars are those classic examples of automotive excellence which combine technical standards with that indefinable spark of genius which some enthusiasts have termed 'head-turning-ability'. It is that ability which has created the great cars of our century. They are cars which have somehow managed to combine the solid merits of engineering with the grace and beauty normally associated with works of art.

It would remain impossible to mention all the dream cars of the past which dominate conversation whenever enthusiasts gather, but some stand head and shoulders, or grill and bonnet, above the others. The great Bentley Blower, more properly termed the 4.5 litre Supercharged Bentley, or the 540K Mercedes Benz, or the type 37 Bugatti encapsulate many people's ideas of grand sports cars. The Rolls-Royce Silver Ghost embodies the taste and elegance of early luxury cars. The Hispano-Suizas epitomised the Continental grace of the pre World War I days. Later cars too count as classics, great cars such as the Lamborghinis and Jaguars rank with the best ever built. Less ostentatious sports cars have proliferated over the years, allowing those with more modest pockets to indulge their dreams in MGs, Triumphs and Fiats.

Whatever the dream, there is a car to fit. For cars have been the substance of dreams ever since the first horseless carriage rattled its way down the street more than a century ago.

THE NATIONAL MOTOR MUSEUM AT BEAULIEU

Montagu of Beaulieu

SPECTEMUR AGENDO

BEFORE THE BEGINNING

A close study of the history of archeology will fail to disclose any hard evidence of self-propelled prehistoric vehicles. No Cro-Magnon cruisers. No fossilized funny cars. But, as anyone with the slightest bit of imagination can see, prehistoric man's harnessing of fire coupled with the invention of the wheel was nothing more than an early pre-attempt to build a steam-driven automobile. Which leads us to...

THE ACTUAL BEGINNING (REALLY)

Steam as a propulsive force was known to the Chinese as far back as 500 B.C. With the exception of the wind, it was to be the motive power of choice until the late 1800's. The first successful steam-powered vehicle was built by a French army engineer named Nicolas Cugnot in 1770. Just how well it performed is a matter of conjecture, but we do know what it looks like. It has been on display in the Conservatoire National des Arts et Métiers in Paris for over two hundred years. Steam power was also being pursued in the English colonies of America. In 1772, Oliver Evans, a young Delaware farmer, designed a vehicle that would apply "the elastic power of steam for original motion." Since his work was interrupted by the Revolutionary War, he was not able to get a patent for his design until 1787. Because of financial difficulties, Evans was never able to build the steam carriage that he predicted would "outrun the swiftest horse." That goal would be reached by others, but it would take nearly one hundred years.

As the century turned, a Cornish mining engineer named Richard Trevithick began work on a steam-powered road carriage which he successfully drove through London in 1803. While America may have lagged behind in actual production of successful steam vehicles, it *was* ahead in at least one other important area. In 1792 the first toll roads started raking in money for the states of Pennsylvania and Connecticut. The steam carriage finally came into its own in the mid-1800's. One sure sign of its growing importance was the intervention of bureauocratic regulators. The British "Red Flag Act" of 1863 was typical. It decreed that all "road locomotives" must have a man walking ahead of them waving a red flag to warn the unwary populace. These flag wavers, known as Naderites, exist to this day working diligently to make the world safe for themselves and assorted Luddites. By the end of the century the use of steam as a motive power was confined more and more to railway engines. In truth, steam-powered automobiles were difficult to start and a maintenance headache—problems that would be solved easily over time. But the advent of the gasoline-powered internal combustion engine meant that the steam engine's time had run out. It is interesting to note that the failure of steam and electric motive power was not due to lack of performance. Between 1898 and 1906 each set a number of official World Land Speed Records, culminating with a run of 121.57 mph by a Stanley Steamer at Daytona Beach, Florida, on January 23, 1906.

Remnants of automotive steam power would continue on into the twentieth century, championed by eccentric geniuses like the Stanley twins, Rollin White and Abner Doble. Although steamers were loved by their partisans, they could no more compete with the gasoline-powered machines than could their equally silent counterparts, the electrics. Where did they come from, these noisy, smelly vehicles powered by...

INFERNAL COMBUSTION

Exactly who invented the gasoline propelled automobile will always be a matter of debate, with claimants from many countries seeking the title. But if we ask who first built such a machine, successfully tested and then marketed it, the answer is Carl Benz. He completed his first three-wheeler in 1885 and began selling it commercially in 1888.

Another German engineer, Gottlieb Daimler, completed the first practical four-wheeled horseless carriage in 1886. Powered by a 1.1 horsepower, single-cylinder engine, it was capable of speeds up to 10 mph.

When we talk about horseless carriages it is because they were just that: a carriage designed to be pulled by a team of horses and modified by the addition of an engine for motive power and some sort of tiller for steering. So, while a horseless carriage might be called an automobile, an automobile should not be called a horseless carriage. (I think.) In the United States it was probably George Brayton, in conjunction with George B. Seldon, who built the first workable gasoline horseless carriage in 1872. The machine never went into production and it would be another twenty-three years before America had its first real automobile manufacturer, the Duryea Motor Wagon Company. Made in Illinois by Charles and Frank Duryea, the water cooled, two-cylinder, four-cycle vehicle was capable of running 18 mph. The company slogan was "A Carriage, Not a Machine," which may help to explain why it folded in 1898. But the gasoline-powered automobile was definitely here to stay. Although there were only about a thousand cars on the planet, a car magazine, The Horseless Age, began publication in 1895. This was one year before a young mechanic in Michigan constructed a quadracycle driven by a two-cylinder, four-horsepower engine. It was the first of millions to bear the name of its inventor, Henry Ford.

Back in England, the "Red Flag Act" finally was repealed in 1896 and a speed limit of 12 mph was set. On the Continent speed was something to strive for, not limit, and in 1895 the first motor race took place. Paris to Bordeaux and back—732 grueling miles over roads built for horse horsepower. At the end it was a gasoline-powered Panhard that took the checker at an average speed of 15 mph.

That November, a similar event took place in America when gas, steam and electric cars raced from Chicago to Evanston, Illinois, and back with victory going to a gas-powered Duryea. By then, hundreds of new manufacturers were springing up in practically every country, each clamoring for the public's attention and money. If it would run at all, there was somebody out there to sell it to. Even outdated designs like the Benz three-wheeler continued to sell, with over 2,000 of them still putt-putting around. It's hard to imagine, but even at this late date most people had yet to *see* their first automobile, let alone ride in or drive one. Nor did everyone who'd had the pleasure like what they saw. A *New York Times* editorial of 1889 said "...these new-fangled vehicles. They are unutterably ugly..." They were a little unattractive. But not those of the next generation. These automobiles would be purpose-built products of their times.

MODERN TIMES

The year 1900 was a significant one for the fledgling motor industry. It was the year a great automotive pioneer, Gottlieb Daimler, died and in which the first automobile of the modern era was born. The two events were not unrelated. As the result of negative publicity about racing accidents involving Daimlers, the public began to question the marques' safety. As a consequence, the new car developed by Daimler, Otto Maybach and, to a lesser extent, Frank Jellinek, was put on the market after Daimler's death and named for Jellinek's daughter, Mercedes. (Imagine the repercussions in today's marketplace if her name has been Hortense.)

This first Mercedes was no horseless carriage. Its pressed steel chassis, honeycomb radiator and advanced four-cylinder 35-hp engine made it the first truly modern automobile. Other manufacturers followed suit, and soon many of the names that we recognize today were staking their claims to a place in the history books: Auburn, Austin, Bugatti, Buick,

Cadillac, Chevrolet, Dodge, Fiat, Lancia, Maxwell, Napier, Oldsmobile, Packard, Peugeot, Renault, Rover, Singer, Sunbeam, Talbot, Vauxhall, Wilbury, Yaxa and Zust. This list, though hardly complete, is representative in that some of the marques are still with us, some are gone but have achieved great fame and desirability as collectors' items, while others have simply vanished. In fact, during the first 100 years of automotive history more than 10,000 marques have come and (mostly) gone.

Among the technical innovations introduced during this exciting period were mechanically operated valves, overhead cams, automatic transmissions, electric driving lights, V-2, 4-, 6-, 8- and 12- cylinder engines, and disc brakes. With the exception of computers and space-age composites, almost every element of today's modern car had appeared in some form prior to the outbreak of the first World War.

Undoubtedly the two most significant cars of the period were the Rolls-Royce Silver Ghost and the Model T Ford. Introduced in 1906 and 1908 respectively, they set the standards for all other manufacturers. Strangely enough, each car would remain in production for nineteen years, but the number of cars manufactured tells the true story: 7,876 Silver Ghosts and fifteen plus million Model T's. Two cars, each perfect for what it was and each perfectly different from the other. The Rolls was intended to be the best regardless of cost, while Henry Ford wanted to build the most cars at the least possible cost. When he started building the Model T it sold for $850, but by the time he was cranking them out at a rate of one every hour the cost was down to $260. There is no need to recount the well-known story of Ford's development of the assembly line or to detail the handmade characteristics of the Rolls-Royce.

What is important is that from this point, automobiles would generally be made for either the upper classes or the masses, with the cars most of us own and drive being some variant of the latter. For the world's major automotive manufacturers the trick would be to mass produce class. This need would bring two new forces into play. Forces which, over time, would become as important to the automotive industry as engineering excellence and technical innovation: styling and advertising.

By 1914 the automobile had all but replaced the horse in everyday life. Its ability to move men and equipment rapidly during World War I drove the last nail into the foreclosure sign on the local blacksmith's shop.

By the time the armistice was signed it was an altogether different world. The next two decades would see the incredible highs of the Jazz Age become the bottomless pit of the Great Depression, and end on the brink of an even more destructive world war. And where would the automobile fit in all of this? Everywhere.

THE GOLDEN AGE

Bugatti Royale, Duesenberg SJ, Hispano-Suiza Type 68, Cord L- 29, Isotta-Fraschini Tipo 8A, Pierce Silver Arrow—These are but a few of the dazzling machines produced during the Golden Age. Style, engineering, performance, class—they had it all. Like the Maltese Falcon, they were truly "the stuff that dreams are made of." That none of their manufacturers have survived has in no way diminished their desirability or worth. And, although they were very expensive when new, it is doubtful that any of their creators could have imagined their value today. (Over $9 million in the case of the Royale, for example.)

Obviously not every car built during this period was made to such lofty standards. For every Duesenberg there were thousands of Dodges, as there were Chevys for every Cord. Ultimately it was the Chevys, Fords, Austins, Fiats and other popular mass-produced makes that would survive the financial collapse of 1929 and the years of misery that followed. Just as all cars are not created equal, neither are their

creators. The great cars of the Golden Age were built by men of great, if often unorthodox, vision. Artist/Engineers. Alchemists able to turn base metal into objects of incredible beauty. (Gold, if you consider what they're worth today.) A brief look at two of these automotive alchemists might give some insight into the type of uncompromising genius needed to build these incredible machines, and why probably we never will see their like again.

Ettore Bugatti.
Born into a family of Italian artisans in 1881, Bugatti bought his first vehicle, a motor tricycle, at age sixteen. After making suitable modifications, he drove it in the Paris- Bordeaux race of 1899. By 1901 he had designed and built two four-wheeled cars and at the ripe old age of twenty-one became a designer for the de Dietrich company. This was soon followed by similar work for Peugeot and Isotta-Fraschini. A meeting with a banker named Viscaya led to the funding of his own factory at Molsheim, Alsace-Lorraine, France. It was here that the first of his now legendary cars, the Type-13, was produced in 1911. This car is typical of all Bugattis in that it was a departure from accepted practice, which deemed that fast touring cars should be big, heavy and powerful. Bugatti entered the tiny four- cylinder, 8-valve car in the Grand Prix du Mans where it finished second to one of the behemoth 18-litre Fiats. The success of his cars on the racetrack proved that a small, high revving engine mounted in a chassis with superb roadholding was preferable to sheer bulk and straightline speed. Racing always would play an important role at Bugatti as a development lab for new ideas and as publicity for the marque. The fact that Bugattis won nearly 2,000 races between 1924 and 1927 gives some idea of the free newsprint generated.

Bugatti himself was known as Le Patron. Revered and feared by his customers, he truly did it his way. Hydraulic brakes, for example. Their development meant that manufacturers finally could do away with the balky, unreliable cables in use until then. But not Le Patron. When he persisted in using cable brakes and potential owners had the gall to complain, he informed them that he made his cars to go, not stop. Another typical story concerns the owner who brought his new Bugatti back to the factory for the third time in hopes of finally getting some minor problem fixed, only to be stopped by Le Patron and told not to come back again. All of this only added to the legends that still surround the cars today. Can anyone imagine Henry Ford not selling a car to a man willing to shell out $20,000 (in 1920 dollars) because he didn't like his table manners? Le Patron did, even though the sloppy eater was a Balkan monarch.

In addition to his automobiles, Bugatti raised pigeons, collected horse-drawn carriages, designed watches, safety razors, sailboats and gasoline-powered trains. What he did in his spare time is unrecorded.

The Great Depression was the beginning of the end for the Bugatti. It only remained for the devastation of World War II to finish the job. At the time of his death the founder was still planning for the postwar Bugattis that, without him, could never be Bugattis. He died on August 21, 1947.

"If I succeed in achieving what I am looking for it will certainly be a car, and a piece of machinery, above any criticism."

Errett Lobham Cord
While Bugattis were setting records at racetracks all over Europe in 1924, a young American car salesman was setting records of another sort. Thirty-year-old Errett Lobban Cord was selling the Moon. (This was not like selling the Brooklyn Bridge. The Moon was a car.) In fact, he was so successful at Moon that the directors of the fading Auburn Company asked him to save their bacon by moving their unsold inventory of cars out of the company parking lot. He agreed, but only in exchange for an option to purchase a controlling interest in the company if he was

successful. Figuring they had nothing to lose, Auburn's directors agreed. Before long they had lost their company and their jobs to the man who had repainted their cars in bright colors, added a bit of nickle plating and sold the lot for a tidy profit. E.L. Cord was on his way.

Knowing the cars were underpowered for their now racy appearance, Cord parlayed his profits and acquired the Lycoming Engine Co. Soon Auburns were as fast as they looked. As he told The New York Times, the automobile "has always been and always will be a style vehicle." By 1929 Auburn's net profits had jumped from 5 to 37.5 million dollars. Cord, however, was not one to sit back and watch his money grow.

In 1926 he went into partnership with two brothers who had the skill but not the cash to build great cars. Fred and August Duesenberg took the money and set out to do exactly what their new partner told them to do: Build the best damn car in the world. Although less than 500 Duesenbergs were made, they were equal to the best the world had to offer. Their beautifully crafted straight-8, double overhead cam, 4 valve per cylinder, 265-hp engines were the most powerful of their time. With the addition of a supercharger the power was upped to a staggering 320 hp. In 1935, Ab Jenkins drove a model SJ for 24 hours at an average speed of 134 mph.

Although he was not an engineer, Cord decided in 1929 to help design a car that would carry his own nameplate. One month before the stock market crash the Cord L-29 was introduced to an eager public. Orders for the advanced front-wheel drive machine poured in, but Black Tuesday and all the dark days that followed took their toll on actual sales. As the Depression worsened, Cord spent more and more time trying to hold together his corporate empire. In addition to his car companies he controlled Stinson Aircraft, his own airline and a giant shipbuilding company.

In 1936 he astonished the automotive world yet again when he began producing one of the most popular of all classic cars, the Gordon Buehrig designed Cord 810. A favorite of movie stars such as Jean Harlow and Tom Mix, it was doomed to failure by the same forces that had stopped production of most "specialty" cars. The 2,320th, and last, Cord rolled out of the factory on August 7, 1937. Later that year Cord sold his automotive interests and retired to a life of activity. He manufactured air conditioners, electric fans, freezers, dish washers and kitchen cabinets, sold real estate, mined uranium, ran a radio station and served as Senator from Nevada. Only death could slow him down, and in 1974 at the age of 79, he died. "One of my first principles is to be different," he wrote, "not spectacular or contrary, but different."

Of course there was another side of the Golden Age story. It concerns the rise of giant manufacturers beginning just after the First World War and continuing in one form or another to this day. In the U.S., Ford and General Motors dominated a marketplace that saw sales go from 2 to 4.5 million vehicles between 1920 and 1929. In Britain and on the continent, the story was the same on a slightly smaller scale. There, combined sales of companies such as Austin, Renault, Citroën, Morris and Peugeot totalled in the millions. They too were selling to a populace ready to break loose after long years of war. The availability of affordable automobiles brought a new kind of freedom to the middle classes. For the auto makers, the availability of large sums of money and material no longer needed for the war effort meant increased production to meet the needs of these new customers. New technologies and techniques of manufacture used to make aircraft and armaments meant lighter, stronger, more economical cars could now be made at lower cost. This quickly translated into more sales and greater profits.

If there is one man who personified this type of corporate automotive production, that man is Alfred P. Sloan. As president and chairman of the board from 1923 to 1946, he helped to make General Motors the single largest corporation in the world. Although widely diversified, its automotive divisions (Chevrolet, Pontiac, Oldsmobile, Buick and Cadillac) are the bedrock on which the company was founded, and on which it relies today for its success or failure. Sloan was the first of the super-managers. Preaching a doctrine of decentralization and rule by committee, he presided over the introduction of the annual model change and the advancement of the styling department, under the brilliant Harley Earl, into the decision-making hierarchy.

Under Sloan's leadership was born the concept of consumer upward mobility, defined as a progression through the G.M. automotive divisions. In theory, the young, first-time customer begins his association with the corporation by buying a Chevy, then chooses one of two paths: as his income and station in life rise, so do his automotive purchases, as he goes from Chevy up the ladder to Cadillac. The second path is the one that leads to brand loyalty, in which case the engineering and styling innovations that begin with Buick and Cadillac will filter down in later model years to staunch Olds, Pontiac and Chevy. Effective? You bet. Simple? Only with the 20/20 vision of hindsight. Under Sloan's leadership G.M. outsold every other car maker in the world. "We set out to produce not for the chosen few but for the whole consumer public."

The Golden Age ended with a bang not a whimper when Hitler marched into Czechoslovakia in 1939. Production of consumer automobiles was all but stopped for the next eight years in Europe and from 1941 to 1946 in America.

Would the next postwar period usher in a second Golden Age, or had the vein been exhausted?

SURVIVAL OF THE FATTEST

As millions of men and women were reentering civilian life the world's automobile manufacturers were busy retooling to give them what they wanted – new cars and lots of them. Cars that, in the U.S., would have an average life span of about five years and would soon be built accordingly.

With G.M., Ford and Chyrsler's twelve different nameplates dominating the American market (G.M. alone already had produced 25 million cars) the few smaller firms that had survived the Depression and war years began to form alliances among themselves. Studebaker with Packard. Nash with Hudson. Mergers that would prove totally ineffectual against the power of the Big Three. Two new manufacturers, Kaiser-Frazer and Tucker also set up shop. Kaiser-Frazer managed to produce some interesting cars, but they would disappear in less than a decade. As for Preston Tucker, he was more akin to Cord and Bugatti than to Sloan. Only 51 of his advanced rear-engine, disc-brake, independent suspension cars were completed before he was forced out of business by false rumors of fraud and stock manipulation.

In Europe the urge to merge was also being felt and for much the same reason: survival. But similarities to the American market did not mean similar cars. American cars of the forties and fifties were overweight, underpowered and, for the most part, about as sleek as the apocryphal horse designed by committee. (A horse with tail fins, no doubt.)

In contrast, the cars on the other side of the pond were small, lightweight, economical to operate and intended to be used a bit longer than five years. In 1947 and 1948 three cars wer introduced and each would find enormous success in its country of origin. One of them would turn out to be a world beater. They were the Morris Minor (England), Citroën 2CV (France) and the Volkswagen Beetle (West Germany).

As has been said, great cars are the product of great minds, and the Morris Minor is another example of this. Conceived by Alec Issigonis during the final years of the war, the Morris Minor was the right car at the right time. Correctly predicting that gas would not become plentiful in Britain for a number of years, he opted for a small, economy car featuring unibody construction and independent front suspension. The car was an immediate success and went on to sell more than a million units. The significance of the car cannot be underestimated. If it had proven a flop, it is doubtful Issigonis would have been permitted to produce the most successful British car of all time, the Mini.

In France both Renault and Citroën introduced small, practical cars in 1947. The rear- engine Renault 4CV, with sales of over a million, was influenced by Ferdinand Porsche's designs for the Volkswagen Beetle. The Citroën 2CV, or Deux Chevaux, looks like it was designed by somebody under the influence. This car, variants of which are still being produced, is the closest thing to the Model T in price, economy and ease of maintenance that exists in our high-tech world. With its original 8 hp engine it had a top speed of 34 mph and got 65 miles to the gallon. Within five years of its introduction Citroën was turning them out at a rate of 1,000 a day and it still wasn't enough to fill all the orders. Strangely enough, the 2CV is now a favorite of the same Hollywood types that once went for Cords and Duesenbergs. Over five million produced and still counting. *Vive la Deux Chevaux!*

The popularity of these cars and others like the Fiat Topolino, Austin A30 and Panhard Dyna didn't mean much to the bean counters in Detroit. After all, why build small, ugly, underpowered cars that got great gas mileage when you could make a lot more money selling large, ugly, underpowered cars that got lousy mileage? It was the Volkswagen that would begin to change that type of thinking. Designed by a genius at the behest of a madman, it would become the most popular car in the history of motoring. Ferdinand Porsche (the genius) was already one of Europe's top designer/engineers, and had done a lot of preliminary work on small prototype rear-engined cars. So, when Adolf Hitler (guess who?) asked Porsche to design a Volkswagen, or "people's car", that every German family could afford, Porsche was ready. The car was introduced at the Berlin Auto Show in 1935 and almost immediately orders began to pour in. By 1938 more than 250,000 Germans had placed orders accompanied by enough down payments to help construct a factory to build the car. Then Hitler decided to start World War II, and although 70,000 VW's were built between 1939 and 1945 they were all military versions. Almost as soon as the surrender agreement was signed the assembly lines began to move, and by the time the Morris Minor and Citroën 2CV were introduced, Volkswagen already had sold 25,000 Beetles. It is still selling them.

On February 17, 1972, when number 15,007,034 rolled off the line, the long-standing record of the Model T was finally broken. Now manufactured in countries such as Mexico and Brazil, the car has passed the twenty million mark.

Needless to say, none of this crossed anyone's mind when the first VW arrived in the States in 1949. Objects of scorn to all but their purchasers, only about a thousand were sold over a four-year period. But the Germans hung in and drove a wedge into the American market that opened the way for a blitzkreig of imports.

What do you do for an encore once you've made a great car for all of the people? You make a great car for some of the people, put your name on it and join the ranks of the world's top performance car constructors. Just like the man from Modena, Il Commendatore, Enzo Ferrari.

What Bugatti was to the aficionados of the twenties and thirties, Enzo Ferrari was to the fifties, sixties, seventies and eighties. From the time of the first Ferrari car in 1947 to his death in 1988 at the age of ninety, his was the name that symbolized speed with style to post- war generations. Even in fifties' America, where conformity was the true religion, the name Ferrari made many hearts beat faster. Fortunately, a few of them happened to be in the bodies of G.M. and Ford engineers, who translated their passion into the Corvette and Thunderbird. For the most part, though, fifties' American cars were exercises in styling excess. When in doubt, add bigger fins and more chrome. Garish? You bet. But people really liked the looks of those cars (except the Edsel). In the eighties, those that survived grew more valuable every day, and cars that seemed laughable at the time now radiate with a warm nostalgic glow (except the Edsel).

The influence of VW and other economy cars did cause some ripples in Detroit. Kaiser-Frazer was the first to respond with the Henry-J, but sales weren't there, and soon neither was the Henry-J. American Motors tried the Rambler, Ford the Falcon and G.M. the Corvair. The first two were fairly successful, although dull and uninspiring, but the Corvair was a beauty. European-influenced styling, coupled with an air- cooled rear-engine and four-wheel independent suspension, made it the most interesting American car since the 1930's. Unfortunately the wrong people became interested in it for the wrong reasons, and it disappeared after a campaign of negative publicity reminiscent of the recent unintended acceleration fiasco.

In reality, Americans still wanted big cars and that's exactly what they got. The true small car revolution would come later, in reaction to the increasing flow of foreign cars and the decreasing flow of foreign oil. And where would the majority of those imports come from? Surely not from some small, overcrowded, smog-laden island in the far reaches of the Pacific Ocean!

Some industry analysts were already warning the major auto makers to wake up and face what was happening in the outside world. Few listened, preferring instead to dream a dream where good guys always won and they were always those guys.

ASLEEP AT THE WHEEL

The first Japanese imports were certainly not likely to cause many sleepless nights in the suburbs of Detroit or Coventry. Made for the home market, they had few of the amenities taken for granted by Western consumers and none of the styling. But the same determination that led to Japanese domination of the computer chip and consumer electronics industries would change all that. By the early 1960's both Datsun (Nissan) and Toyota had begun to appeal to young buyers who saw them as an affordable alternative to the Beetle.

In 1960 imports accounted for about ten percent of the American market with comparable sales for U.S.-built compacts. But by 1963 the proliferation of choices offered by Detroit, 429 different models that year alone, cut the imports by half. Then, the following year Detroit rediscovered performance with the arrival of two hot new cars: the Pontiac GTO and Ford Mustang.

The GTO was nothing more than a run-of-the-mill compact Tempest with bigger brakes, stiffer springs and a monster 400-cubic-inch V-8 stuffed under the hood. It could really move. Suddenly tail fins were out and 0 to 60 elapsed time was king.

The success of the first "muscle" car was soon topped by the arrival of the first "pony" car. The Ford Mustang was affordable, practical and truly exciting to a whole new generation of drivers. Soon there were Firebirds, Superbirds, Barracudas, Camaros and Chargers blasting away from stoplights all across the country. Talk of economy was replaced by discussions of cubic inches, fat tires and higher insurance rates.

It's interesting to note that three of the most memorable postwar cars to come out of Detroit, the Corvette, Mustang and GTO were associated with individuals within the corporate structure: Zora Arkus-Duntov, Lee Iacocca and John De Lorean.

In Britain the industry was moving even further toward large manufacturing entities. But, unlike America, there was still room for the small specialty car maker. Most had very little effect on the automotive world as a whole while others, like Colin Chapman, became international figures. A brilliant engineer, he built the first Lotus racing car in 1949. The road cars, from the 1958 Elite to the current Esprit Turbo, are among the world's best. His sudden death in 1982 at the age of fifty-four meant that there was one less innovator to hold back the rising tide of imitators. Lotus is now owned by G.M., for whom it functions as a research and development facility. Computer controlled "active" suspension systems and other hi-tech innovations that will appear on mass-produced cars within the next few years are among the products being perfected there.

On the Continent the story was much the same. Even Enzo Ferrari was accepting suitors, among them Henry Ford II. But it was Fiat that gained the prize in 1969, becoming the majority shareholder, yet leaving control in Ferrari's hands. Lee Iacocca, who was instrumental in Ford's unsuccessful Ferrari bid, would have better luck at Chrysler, buying major interests in both Maserati and Lamborghini.

By the time of the Chrysler deal, Feruccio Lamborghini had been gone from the company bearing his name for more than ten years. Unlike Bugatti or Ferrari, Lamborghini was not personally identified with his cars. He had made his fortune manufacturing tractors, commercial heating units and air conditioners. A true enthusiast who once raced in the Mille Miglia, he always kept a stable of exotic high-performance cars. Unhappy with the workmanship on one of his Ferraris, he decided to drive to Maranello and speak to Enzo about it. After cooling his heels for a few hours in a waiting room outside Il Commendatore's office, he realized that Ferrari had no intention of seeing him. The angry Lamborghini who stormed away was no longer just another rich Italian industrialist. Feruccio Lamborghini's anger had transformed him into a car maker whose avowed goal was to beat Ferrari at his own game by producing the ultimate high- performance exotic.

His first car, the quad cam, V-12, GT-350, appeared in 1964. It was followed over the years by other, even more exciting creations: Islero, Jarama, Espada, Muira, Urraco and finally in 1974 by the head-turningest, eye-poppingest car in the universe, the Countach. Unfortunately, by the time it was introduced, Lamborghini was no longer associated with the company. Financial and other pressures from his industrial empire prompted him to sell, but not before he had overseen development of the car with which, in many people's opinion, he fulfilled his dream of outdoing Ferrari.

In 1973, while the prototype Countach was roaring up and down the Milan-Turin Autostrada, another event was taking place that would have far greater effect on the motoring world. The price of crude oil went from three to twelve dollars a barrel. While the effects of this were felt worldwide, it had its greatest impact in the land of the turnpike and home of the gas guzzler, where panicked legsislators tried everything short of reviving the Red Flag Act to make the problem go away.

WHAT GOES AROUND

The years following the oil embargo panic of 1973 have seen changes in the automotive industry that will be with us well into the next century. Tougher fuel economy, safety and emission control requirements mandated by more and more governments have resulted in more efficient, safer and, yes, better cars. But the cost of implementing these changes has been tremendous and, as always, has been passed along to the consumer. Ford, for example, spent more money in 1978 developing cars to meet the new requirements than the entire amount they'd spent for development of every car since Henry built the first one on his kitchen table. Even a Yugo or Hyundai carries a higher sticker price today than the Cord L-29 did when it was introduced. Talk about inflation!

Today's cars are designed with the aid of computers, built with the help of industrial robots and styled in a wind tunnel. They go faster, stop quicker and last longer, but there is a similarity to all of them no matter what their nameplate or country of origin. If they *have* a definable country of origin. When Ford introduced the Escort in 1980 they called it "the world car." Designed in Europe, it is assembled in various countries, utilizing a Japanese transmission and running gear. An instant success, it continually outsells all other cars in the world. Yet compared to the confused international pedigrees of some cars, it is actually somewhat parochial. The new Ford Mustang of 1986 was designed around a Japanese chassis, assembled by a Mazda factory in America and is powered by an American Ford engine. Ford obviously has come a long way since Henry II declared he'd never have a "Jap engine" under the hood of a car with his name on it.

As a way to overcome the restrictive import quotas placed on their cars by worried foreign governments, the Japanese car makers simply followed the lead of Volkswagen and began making their cars in those same countries. Perhaps the most successful of these is Honda, which opened its first plant in the U.S. in 1982 and within four years had become the fourth largest maker of cars in the country. The worldwide success of Honda must, to a great extent, be attributed to its founder and leader, Soichiro Honda. As a motorcycle manufacturer he always was considered an outsider by the leaders of the Japanese auto industry. Nonetheless, he is the only Japanese auto maker who is readily identified with his cars. Is this because they are made with such outstanding quality and engineering *or* could it be the other way around?

Today's automobiles are still designed and built by human brains and hands, but the builders themselves are becoming more and more anonymous. In all probability the day of the entrepreneurial carmaker has come to a close. Recent attempts, such as the Bricklin or the ill-fated De Lorean DMC-12, can only emphasize the difficulties that must be overcome in order to get a new car off the drawing board. There are still a great many specialty firms, but they are mostly kit-car builders or aftermarket rebuilders. Firms like Koenig, Ruf, AMG and Calloway take high-performance cars and push them that one extra step that makes them unique. The thought that someone can improve the performance of a Ferrari Testarossa or Porsche 911 Turbo is awe inspiring. Fifty years ago such a person probably would have been building his own car from the ground up.

What does the future hold? More of the same, and less. Future cars will become even more efficient, but at some point, as fossil fuel supplies dwindle away, our old friend the gasoline-powered internal combustion engine will have to go. Its replacement? Solar power? Electric power? Maybe even steam power will make a comeback. Whatever form the car of the future takes, you can bet the breakthrough will be made by a person, not a corporation. Someone who will be written about in a hundred years the way Benz, Ford and Bugatti are written about here. Someone with a passion for cars who can say, as designer Harley Earl did, "I dream automobiles."

1, 3 & 5 1966 AC SHELBY COBRA 427 S/C
Sixty-two years before this 7-litre barn burner began setting records on the racetrack, the Auto Carrier Company was known for manufacturing small, efficient delivery vans. It wasn't until 1907, with the production of a passenger car, that the initials AC were adopted. One can only hope that the first car, the Sociable, lived up to its name as well as the 500hp Cobra did. **2 1982 AC ME3000** This interesting car began life in 1972 as a one-off special called the Diablo. One of its designers was responsible for the movie car, Chitty-Chitty Bang-Bang. AC bought the rights to the design and began production in 1978. **4 1960 AC GREYHOUND** In October 1960 AC began production of the four seat Greyhound. Derived from the sportier Aceca, the first Greyhounds were plagued with bad handling due to problems in the rear suspension , but this was soon corrected. **6 1966 SHELBY COBRA 427 S/C IN RACING TRIM**

1

2

3

4

5

6

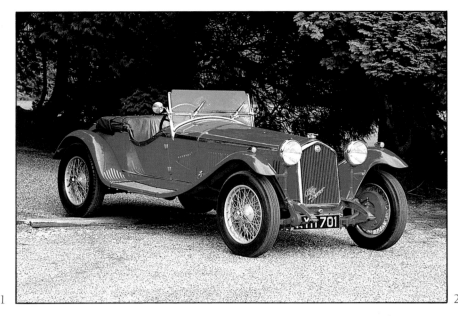

1

2

3

4

1 1931 ALFA ROMEO 6C 1750 The 6C 1750 was designed by the great Vittorio Jano. In production from 1929 to 1933, it is considered by many to be the most perfect Alfa ever made. **2, 4, 6 & 7 ALFA ROMEO 8C 2900B** In an effort to continue their dominance of long distance sports car racing, Alfa increased the size of their engines to 2.9 litres, first with the 8C 2900A, and then, in 1937, with the 8C 2900B. In 1938 a team of four 8C 2900B's set out on the Mille Miglia and at the conclusion of the thousand mile race were placed one, two and three. **3 1932 ALFA ROMEO 8C 2300** Jano's next Alfa design was this 8C 2300, introduced in 1931. **5 ALFA ROMEO 6C 2500** Just before the outbreak of World War II Alfa Romeo began to manufacture the 6C 2500. One of the last models built was a special order roadster by Touring for Benito Mussolini. After the war, a number of the surviving 6C 2500 chassis were fitted with new coachwork by Touring (now officially Carrozzeria Touring Superleggera), Pininfarina and Boneschi. It's said that whenever an Alfa passed him by, Henry Ford tipped his hat. Looking at these cars, it's not hard to see why.

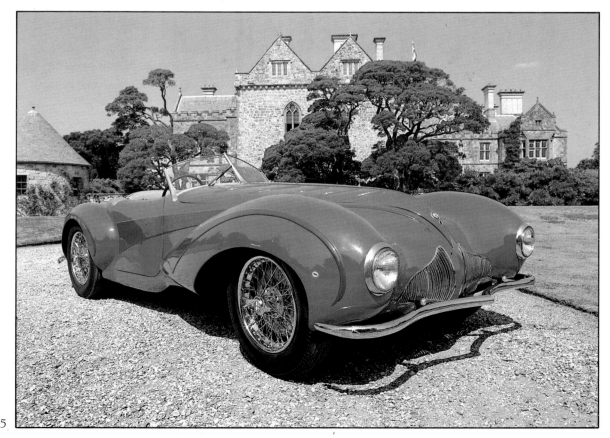

5

6

7

1, 2, & 5 1955 ALFA ROMEO B.A.T. 9d The B.A.T. series began in 1953 when Nuccio Bertone's company was commissioned by Alfa Romeo to design a special showcarbody on its Model 1900 chassis. The final evolution of the design was the 1955 B.A.T.9d. **3 1974 ALFA ROMEO 1600 SPYDER** Introduced in 1967 and still produced today, the Spyder along with the Porsche 911 holds the record as the world's longest produced sports car. Powered by a 4 cyl., aluminium twin cam,this car, in all of its versions, is the closest most of us will ever get to true classic sports car ride and handling. **4 1959 ALFA ROMEO GUILIETTA 1300 SPYDER** In the 50's and 60's the Guilia and Guilietta were Alfa's bread and butter cars. They were affordable, fairly reliable *and* they were real sports cars. **6 1984 ALFA ROMEO GTV 6 2+2** This sohc 2492cc V-6 engined car features a microprocessor-controlled digital ignition system for increased performance and more efficient fuel expenditure. **7 1989 ALFA ROMEO 75** The Alfa 75 (the Milano in the U.S.) was a welcome replacement for the GTV. Available with 2-, 2.5-, and 3-litre power, it is the last true Alfa in the classic mold. **8 1989 ALFA ROMEO 75 TWIN SPARK ENGINE**The 4 cyl., 2-litre twin spark has two valves and two plugs per cylinder.

3

4

5

6

7

8

1

2

3

4

1 & 2 1936 & 1937 ALVIS SPEED 25 The first Alvis, the 10/30, was produced in 1920. The company made many interesting cars over the years, including a series of front-wheel-drive cars in the late 1920's, as typified by the 1928 model shown here (**4**). But it is the 3.5 litre Speed 25 which is considered by many to be the best produced by the marque. **5 1963 ALVIS TD 21** This Alvis, with its classic Mulliner-Park Ward coachwork,was one of the last to be produced before the company was sold to Rover in 1965. By 1967 Alvis had ceased production altogether. **3 1948 ALLARD** Designed and built by Sydney Herbert Allard, these cars were as much at home on the race-track as on the highway. Powered by a Ford V-8, this K1 convertible was the predecessor of the 1952 Monte Carlo winning P1 sedan.

5

6

7

9

8

6 1935 ARMSTRONG SIDDELEY, 7 1946 ARMSTRONG SIDDELEY TYPHOON, 8 1960 ARMSTRONG SIDDELEY SAPPHIRE Armstrong Siddeley was the car of choice not of enthusiasts but of doctors, clergymen and little old gray haired ladies. This may explain why they were among the first automakers to offer an automatic transmission, the "self changing" gearbox. Capitiziing on their wartime production of aircraft they named their first postwar models the Lancaster, Hurricane and Typhoon. The last and most famous model was the Sapphire, a 3.4 litre which began production in 1952 and continued until the company went out of the automobile business in 1960. **9 1972 AMERICAN MOTORS AMX** The AMX was intended to bring new, younger buyers, into American Motors showrooms. A true performance car, it set a number of Land Speed Records during its first year of availability in 1968. Sales were disappointing and in 1970 the two seat AMX was replaced by the four passenger Javelin.

1 & 2 1932 ASTON MARTIN LE MANS The Le Mans evolved from the New International. Available in two- or four- seat configurations, it was an immediate success with motoring critics as well as the public. The car was heavy (2350 lbs.) for its 70hp engines, but offered superb roadholding. **3 1950 ASTON MARTIN DB-2** Although fitted with a production type body this car was powered by the Bentley designed, 6 cyl., LB6 engine. **4 ASTON MARTIN DB-3S ENGINE** These 2922cc engines developed between 182 and 240hp. They powered their way to wins in races throughout Europe and Great Britain from 1953 through 1956. **5 1981 ASTON MARTIN DBS V-8** The 5.3 litre V-8 first appeared in 1970 and has become the 'standard' model of the marque. These are powerful cars capable of speeds approaching 140mph even when equipped with automatic transmission.

1

2

3

4

5

**ASTON MARTIN VANTAGE V-8 (9),
ZAGATO (6), AND VOLANTE (7)**
Cars in the Vantage series are
high-performance refinements of the standard
V-8. Their 5.3 litre, 240hp engines offer incredible
torque and a top speed of 170mph. This
performance goes hand in hand with superb
craftsmanship to make them among the most
desirable cars in the world. **8 1982 ASTON
MARTIN LAGONDA** First produced in 1978, the
Lagonda presented a fascinating combination
of Old World tradition and space age
technology, featuring touch sensitive switches
and digital instrument readouts that were truly
state of the art, juxtaposed with a hand-shaped
aluminium body. The Lagonda is still being built
to much the same specifications and in much
the same manner. It takes four months and
1,800 man hours to make each of them.

6

7

8

9

1 & 2 1931 and 1935 AUBURN PHAETON SEDANS
As we learned in the Introduction, it was a parking lot ful lof Auburns that started E.L. Cord on his way into the history books. But what about the cars themselves? Always overshadowed by both Duesenberg and Cord, they were still, as their popular slogan put it, "A lot of car for the money." The phaetons shown here typified one style of Auburn, while the boattail V-12 (**4**) is a perfect example of what many considered the 'baby' Duesenberg. With sales dropping from a high of 31,000 in 1931 to only 4,800 in 1933 the writing was on the wall. The final Auburns were designed by Alan Leamy for 1934 and refined by Gordon Buehrig for '35 and '36. By then the books showed nothing but red ink and within the year the Auburn was gone.

1

2

3

4

5

6

7

8

**5 1984 AUDI 80 QUATTRO
6 1986 AUDI QUATTRO 7 1985 AUDI
200 QUATTRO TURBO ENGINE 8 1985 AUDI
QUATTRO SPORT 9 1988 AUDI 80 1.8e** Rising
from the ashes of the pre- World War II
Auto-Union Company, the first Audi was
produced in 1963 under the supervision of
former Mercedes Benz Grand Prix car designer
Ludwig Kraus. When Kraus retired, development
was taken over by Ferdinand Piech, grandson of
the great Ferdinand Porsche. With this lineage it
is no wonder that Audi has become a world
beater in rally competition with its full time,
four-wheel-drive model, the Quattro. Powered
by a unique 5 cyl. engine, the Quattro has
proven to be one of the performance cars of
the decade since its introduction in 1980. As it
has evolved, options such as turbocharging, ABS
braking and, beginning in 1987, a 4 cyl. engine
have become available. Newer Quattros
feature the Torsen (torque sensing) center
differential. This automatically boosts the torque
of whichever wheels offer the best traction.
Current models are powered by a 130hp, 5 cyl.,
coupled with a 5-speed manual transmission.
The larger model Quattros have a 162hp,
2.2-litre turbo (**7**). The shape of the 80/90 series (**9**)
offers one of the lowest coefficient of drag (Cx)
figures of any sedan in the world.

9

1

2

3

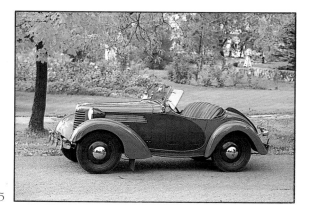

4

5

6

1 1925 AUSTRO-DAIMLER Manufactured from 1899 to 1934, Austro-Daimler was fortunate in having the services of designer Ferdinand Porsche, who developed many of their earlier cars before departing in 1923. **2 1927 AUSTIN SEVEN "CHUMMY"** Although Austin had been producing cars since 1906, including a number of Grand Prix cars based on standard sedans like the one pictured here (**3**), it was the Austin Seven that really put the company on the map. Introduced in 1922, it went against the prevailing concept of small cars being cycle based. The Seven was essentially a scaled down larger car with a quiet, reliable 747cc, 10.5hp engine capable of 50mph. The standard "Chummy" four seat aluminium body was augmented many times over the years, as can be seen in the American produced Bantam Roadster of 1939 (**5**). Sixteen years in production, the Seven obviously was doing something right. The Austin Ten, shown here in a 1935 Colwyn Cabriolet version(**4**), was Austin's best selling car throughout the 30's and stayed in production until 1947. The 2.3 litre Model Sixteen (**6**) was a smaller version of the 6-cyl. Model Twenty. The Mini, (**9**) along with the

Model T and VW Beetle, is one of the most important and successful small cars ever produced. The first Austin version (it was produced by a number of manufacturers) was called the Seven in honor of their earlier car. The Mini has been in continuous production since its introduction in 1959. By the time the 1981 example pictured here was produced, more than 4.5 million already had preceeded it. **7 1958 AUSTIN HEALEY SPRITE** Unveiled in 1958, the Sprite was an immediate success. Its 4cyl., 1048cc, 42hp engine moved the tiny car along at 80mph. The Sprite was produced until 1971, by which time it was virtually indistinguishable from its counterpart, the MG Midget. **8 1965 AUSTIN HEALEY 3000 MARK THREE** Produced between 1959 and 1968, the 3000 was the last of the Austin Healey line, which began 1955. Its 148hp, 6-cyl., 2912cc engine gave the car a top speed of 120mph.

7

8

9

10

1

2

3

1 **1954 BRISTOL 404** Aircraft quality construction made the 2 litre Bristol 404 one of the most desirable sports cars of its era. Its light aluminium body mated to a solid 96 inch wheelbase chassis was yet another refinement of the 1930's BMW design. **3 1930 BUGATTI TYPE 41 ROYALE** The ultimate luxury car from the ultimate carmaker. Six Type 41 chassis were made and each of them is now worth a king's ransom. One of the six, chassis 41 141, recently was auctioned for 9.7 million dollars. The Royale pictured here, chassis 41 150, is thought to be the last produced. The duplex cabriolet (or double berline de voyage) was built at Bugatti's own factory coachworks. For a car like this, specs are meaningless. The Bugatti Royale may be the ultimate dream car. **4 1932 BUGATTI TYPE 55 SUPER SPORTS** If you can't quite justify buying a Royale, perhaps a Type 55 will do. Derived from Bugatti's racing cars, the Type 55 was powered by a blown dohc, 2.3 litre Type 51 Grand Prix engine set in a Type 54 Grand Prix chassis with coachwork by Figoniet Falaschi.

4

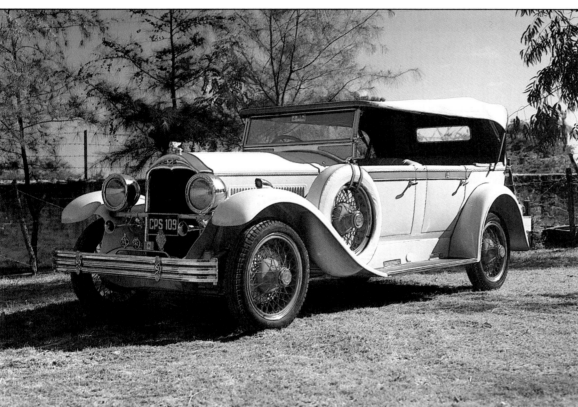

5 1912 BUICK ROADSTER
Scottish-born David Dunbar Buick
built the first Buick automobile in 1903. By the
time this roadster, with its three-speed sliding-
gear transmission was made, Buicks were selling
at the rate of 25,000 per year and Walter P.
Chrysler was running the company. **6 1951
BUICK SUPER EIGHT** The 1951 Super was
powered by a 263.3ci, 120hp straight eight. It
was available with a three-speed manual
transmission, but most buyers opted for the
Dynaflow automatic version. **7 1928
MCLAUGHLIN-BUICK** This touring car is one of
many manufactured in Canada by the
McLaughlin Motor Car Company, utilizing Buick
running gear and McLaughlin coachwork. The
car is one of two seven passenger, long
wheelbase, Master Six tourers constructed for
the use of the Prince of Wales during an official
visit to Toronto. **8 1938 BUICK SPECIAL** The '38
Special's 107hp "Dynaflash" engine was able to
propell the car to better than 90mph. This
example, sports custom Albemarle coachwork
by Carlton. **10 1930 BUICK SERIES 40 PHAETON**
Only 1,100 of these four passenger Phaetons
were built in1930.

1 1930 4.5 LITRE "BLOWER" BENTLEY Only 50 of these brutal looking machines were built, yet they are probably the best known model produced by the marque. The crank driven, Roots-type supercharger, or blower, juts out of the front of the car like the bowsprit of a windjammer. The engine that was being blown had a single overhead cam, four valves per cylinder and dual magnetos firing dual spark plugs. In race trim it developed 240hp and pushed the heavy car to speeds well in excess of 100mph. **2 1928 BENTLEY 4.5 TOURER** The 4.5 tourer was capable of speeds in the 95 to 100mph range. This is one of eight specially built short wheelbase models. **3 1926 BENTLEY 3 LITRE VANDEN PLAS** Probably the most popular of all the Bentley models, the 3litre would remain in production until 1929, by which time 1,619 had been sold.

4 & 5 TWO 1935 BENTLEY 3.5's W.O.
Bentley, like every other maker of fine
(expensive) automobiles, was hard hit by the
market crash of 1929. He lost control of his
company, which was then bought by Rolls-
Royce in 1931. The first of the new Rolls-Royce
built Bentleys, the 3.5, appeared in 1933. The
two cars illustrated here, a standard saloon and
drophead coupe, are typical examples of the
3.5. **6 1936 BENTLEY 4.5 VANDEN PLAS
CONVERTIBLE** In 1936 the 3.5 litre engine was
replaced by the Rolls-Royce 25/30 4.5 litre. This
model would remain in production until the
outbreak of World War II. **7 1930 BENTLEY 8 LITRE
SALOON W.O.** Bentley's final creation was the
magnificent 8 litre. With a top speed of 105mph
this was truly a grand tourer, particularly when
fitted with elegant coachwork, like this example
from H.J.Mulliner.

4

5

6

7

1

2

3

4

5

1 1955 BENTLEY S-TYPE 1955 The S-Type's first year was 1955. The car had a new chassis but utilized the existing R-Type engine and shared its standard body with the Rolls-Royce Silver Cloud. **2 1951 BENTLEY MK VI** Utilizing the same engine as the postwar Rolls-Royce Silver Wraith, the MK VI was a powerful car for its relatively small size. On its introduction in 1946 *The Autocar* called it "a fast turning, hill devouring vehicle." **3 1957 BENTLEY CONTINENTAL S.1** This replacement for the popular R-Type Continental was longer, wider and 550 pounds heavier. Although still capable of 120mph speeds, the Continental was losing its sporting feel. Most of its buyers, in fact, opted for the automatic transmission version. The beautiful coachwork by H.J.Mulliner belied the car's larger dimensions and increasingly pedestrian character. **4 1959 BENTLEY CONTINENTAL S.1** Compare this example with the Mulliner-bodied Continental

6

S.1. Same model. Same mechanicals. Totally different car. **5 1935 BENTLEY 3.5 SPORTS SALOON** Another version of the first Rolls/Bentley as seen in 29-4 and 29-5. **6 1956 BENTLEY CONTINENTAL S.1** This Park Ward convertible is yet another variation on the Continental S.1 theme. Like all S.1's, its 4887cc, R-Type engine featured an improved cylinder head design to help it go, and a fully hydraulic braking system to help it stop. **7, 8 & 9 BENTLEY TURBO R** The Turbo R and its predecessor, the Mulsanne Turbo, represent a serious and successful attempt to regain Bentley's long-lost sporting image. A luxurious burled walnut and Connolly leather interior coupled with fully independent suspension, rack and pinion steering and an engine capable of a 140+ mph top speed place the two Turbo Bentley's among the world's fastest luxury touring cars.

7

8

9

1

2

1 1973 BMW 3.0 csi COUPE A development of the 1970 2800 cs, the 3.0 csi offered a 200hp, Bosch injected engine capable of 137mph when coupled with the Getrag manual gearbox. The 3.0 csi ceased production in 1974. Today, this model is considered a desirable, affordable collectible. **2 1938 BMW 328** Introduced in 1937, the 328 was destined to become a sought-after classic. After the war the 328 designs were taken over by the British and the engine was used in various versions by Frazer Nash, Bristol, Cooper, Lister and AC. **3 1985 BMW M535i** With its 3.4 litre, 4 valve six that produces 286hp, the M535i is capable of hauling itself and its passengers along the autobahn at 155mph. **4 1987 BMW 325i** In 1987 the 3-series BMW's introduced a new type catalytic converter system that produced a 45+ horsepower gain in all models. On the 325i, that translates to a 0 to 60 of 8 seconds and a top speed of 130mph. The convertible version has proven to be the most popular of the 325i's. **5 1987 BMW M-3** A homologation special (that

3

4

5

6

7

means that a certain number must be built in order for the model to qualify as a production-class race car, the M-3 is a purpose built racer that can be driven on the street by those fortunate enough to get their hands on one. Powered by a 195hp, twin-cam, 16 valve, inline 4 that's based on the BMW F1 engine, the 147 mph M-3 is a wolf in wolf's clothing. **6 1986 BMW M-635 csi** The BMW M-6 series cars are luxury grand tourers meant to compete with the Mercedes 500 series and Jag XJS. **7 1988 BMW 750il** Is this the ultimate modern grand touring car? If not, then its about as close as anybody has come. An aluminium 60-degree sohc V-12 moves the 4090 lb 750il effortlessly from 0 to 60 in 7.5 seconds, then cruises along the highway (make that autobahn) at 155 mph. A special ZF 4-speed automatic allows manual shifting if you find yourself at a stop light next to an AMG Hammer. **8 1985 BMW M-1** Only 439 were made. Of that number 400 were road cars for homologation purposes and 39 were race cars. Designed by Girogetto Giugiaro's Ital Design, the M-1 first appeared in 1976. All 439 of you know what it's really like. The rest of us hate your guts.

8

1 1949 BUICK ROADMASTER SEDANET The four portholes in the fender identify this Buick as a Roadmaster (Supers only rated three). **2 1963 BUICK RIVIERA** When the Buick Riviera debuted in 1949 it offered a new styling innovation, a pillarless hardtop. **3 1954 BUICK SUPER CONVERTIBLE** That's right, three portholes. Behind the portholes a 170hp V-8 was the motive force for this car, which owed much of its styling to the famed 1953 Skylark. **4 1955 BUICK CENTURY CONVERTIBLE** In 1955, Buick upped the horsepower of the 322ci Century to 236. Again the "look" is derived from the Skylark. **5 1953 BUICK SKYLARK** Buick's Golden Anniversary was in 1953, and to celebrate the occasion they introduced the limited edition, $5,000, Skylark V-8 convertible. Only 1,690 were made and they are much sought after by collectors. **6 1989 BUICK REATTA** Just as the Skylark caused a stir in Buick showrooms, so too did the sporty Reatta in 1988. A 165hp, 3.8 litre V-6 coupled with 4-wheel independent suspension and computer assisted anti-lock disc brakes make the Reatta a real contender in the luxury sports car category.

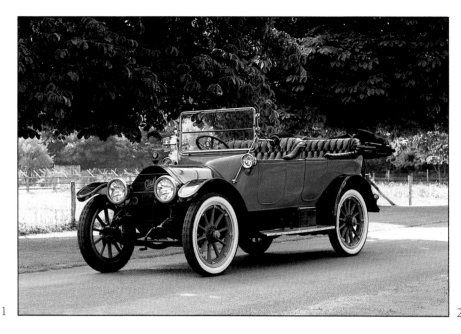

1

2

3

4

1 1913 CADILLAC MODEL 30 TOURER The first Model 30 appeared in 1909 and remained in production through 1914. It was the first American car to offer a closed body as standard equipment, the famous "Body by Fischer." **2 1959 CADILLAC COUPE DE VILLE** The year 1959 may best be remembered for the fact that the Caddy tailfins reached their apogee (or perigee, depending on your point of view). The 390ci Coupe de Ville offered optional air suspension, cruise control, Glide-matic headlight beam control, power door locks, E-Z Eye tinted glass and an automatic finger-touch-tuned, two speaker radio with electrically operated antenna. The tailfins were free. **3 1932 CADILLAC 355B** The 1932 Cadillac 352ci V-8 engine was rated at 115hp. It was mated to a triple-silent, syncro-mesh 3-speed transmission and could reach 75 mph. This was the last year that Cadillac offered buyers a choice of hood ornaments. This example shows the swan rather than the goddess. **4 1931 CADILLAC 355** These V-8 powered cars had coachwork similar to that found on the V-12 that paced the '31 Indianapolis 500. **6 1956 CADILLAC ELDORADO** Though this 365ci, 305hp

5

Eldorado hardly could be called a performance car, it did get around pretty well for its size and weight, managing 0 to 60 in under eleven seconds. The Eldorado was one of Harley Earl's creations, based on the XP-8, XP-9 and XP-300 show cars. The first production Eldorado appeared in 1953. **7 1957 CADILLAC ELDORADO BROUGHAM** For 1957 Eldorado offered an updated engine package: 320hp, twin 4-barrel carbs, special intake manifold and 10 to 1 compression ratio. As for the body, designers on the car were said to have been influenced by the Bristol 404 and Alfa Romeo B.A.T. cars. Interiors were available in standard leather or the more exotic Cape Buffalo. The price for this? A mere $13,074. **8 1959 CADILLAC CONVERTIBLE** Two of the 138,527 Cadillacs produced in 1959, sitting in the sun. **9 1961 CADILLAC FLEETWOOD 75 LIMOUSINE** The 21-foot long 75 limo was constructed on its own special chassis and weighed in at 5,600 pounds.

6

7

8

9

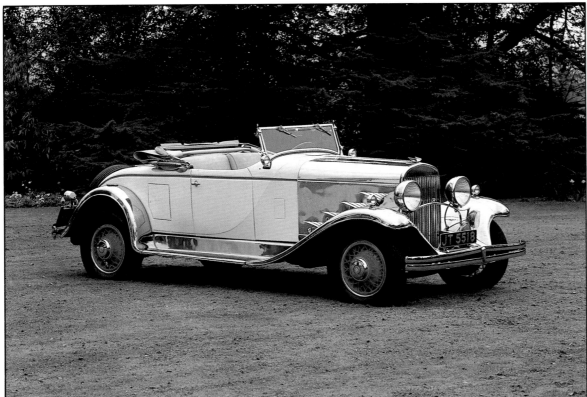

1 1932 CHRYSLER IMPERIAL CH SEDAN For 1932 the Imperial's 384.8ci V-8 engine developed 125hp, managed a 0 to 60 time of 20 seconds and a top speed of 96mph. Chrysler made two separate series of Imperials that year, the CL and the CH, which has a shorter wheel base by eleven inches. **2 1931 CHRYSLER CD CONVERTIBLE COUPE LEBARON** The CD offered Chrysler buyers their first chance at V-8 power. In May the CD series was upgraded to deluxe status, getting a slightly more powerful engine (88hp) and the same rakish split windshields seen on the CD Imperials. **3 1930 CHRYSLER 77 ROADSTER** Powered by an inline 6-cyl, 93hp engine, the sporty 77 roadster, complete with rumble (or dickey) seat, had a 4 speed transmission and the new "Futura" design instrument panel. **4 1933 CHRYSLER CUSTOM IMPERIAL CL** The first year of the top-of-the-line CL series was 1933. This example, a dual-cowl Phaeton by LeBaron, is one of the only eleven produced that year, and is considered one of the most beautiful cars of the period.

5

6

7

8

5 1957 CHRYSLER 300C Introduced in 1954, the 300C was big and brutally fast. It had to be big to handle the power of the famed 331ci Hemi engine that ruled the NASCAR tracks, and it had to be fast since "300" also was its horsepower rating. By 1957 the Hemi, having gobbled up everything in sight, had grown to 392ci, and was putting out 375hp. Top speed was now in the 135mph neighborhood. Nice neighborhood.
6 1941 CHRYSLER NEW YORKER CONVERTIBLE COUPE The New Yorker series cars were one step below the top-of-the-line Imperials. They were equipped with "Spitfire" 8-cyl. engines and fluid drive transmissions. **7 1946 CHRYSLER NEW YORKER CLUB COUPE** Chrysler's heavy involvement with war production meant that its first postwar models would be designs intended for the 1942 model year. **8 1960 CHRYSLER 300F** By the time the 300 had moved down the alphabet to "F" it had lost the Hemi engine and become generally more civilized. A 413ci V-8 rated at 275hp wasn't bad, but it wasn't a Hemi.

1

2

3

4

5

1 1922 CITROËN C3 CLOVERLEAF The Citroën Type C's were small, 856ci, 11hp vehicles that could run 40 mph downhill with a tailwind. Though prized by collectors, the Type C's were not destined for longevity, and the last one was produced in 1926. **2 1959 CITROËN 2CV** Some twenty years after the demise of the tiny Type C, another Citroën appeared that gave new meaning to the term small car. It was called the 2CV. For more than forty years these weird-looking cars have gone about their business of providing cheap, reliable transportation to millions of drivers the world over. **3 1937 CITROËN 7CV TOURER** The Traction Avant (or front-wheel-drive) was André Citroën's last design. **4 1975 CITROËN SM** Unveiled in 1970, the SM (Super Maserati) was a high-performance derivative of the revolutionary Citroën DS (Desirée Spécial). As one of the first production cars to be designed using a wind tunnel, it's not surprising that it has an incredibly low coefficient of drag (0.25). **5 1938 CITROËN TYPE 11 SALOON** Another version of the Traction Avant. This one was built at the firm's British works in Slough.

6 1936 CORD 810 WESTCHESTER SEDAN The car that became the highly prized front-wheel drive Cord 810 began life as a rear-drive, straight eight called the "Baby" Duesenberg. By the time a prototype actually was built, E.L. Cord, in his usual fashion, had changed everything around until it suited him. What suited him was quite a machine. **7 1937 CORD 812 CONVERTIBLE** The 812's supercharged Lycoming V-8 delivered 190hp and would turn an honest 110mph top speed. Ab Jenkins set a number of speed records at Indianapolis and Bonneville in an 812 sedan. The car had a pre-selector gearbox, unit body construction, independent front suspension, and, of course, a supercharger. In two years of production 2,320 810's and 812's were made. Obviously that wasn't enough, since a number of people are making money today by selling fiberglass Cord replicas. **8 & 9 1930 and 1931 Cord L-29** The low, sleek look of the L-29 is due, in part, to E.L.'s decision to use a front-wheel drive design adapted from the Miller Indy race cars. One satisfied owner, Frank Lloyd Wright, had an L-29 for thirty years. He said it looked "becoming" next to his houses.

1 1958 CHEVROLET IMPALA According to Chevrolet's admen, the '58 Impala was endowed with "sculpturamic beauty" that hailed a new era in styling. They also promised buyers "the road smoothingest, nerve smoothingest ride imaginable." Whatever, it must have worked. Sixty thousand of the 250hp V-8 engined Impalas were sold. **2 1969 CORVETTE STINGRAY** The second generation Sting Ray was introduced in 1968, although without the Sting Ray name plate. It was essentially unchanged for '69, but the Stingray name returned (as a single word). **3 1963 CORVETTE STING RAY** The first Sting Ray design was an immediate hit with the public and the automotive press. **4 1978 CORVETTE INDY PACE CAR REPLICA** The year of Corvette's twenty-fifth anniversary, 1978, the car was selected to pace the 62nd Indianapolis 500. The car was labelled a "limited edition," but in reality 6,200 were made, one for each Chevy dealership in the country. Customers waited, to buy them up at prices up to $10,000 over the $13,653 sticker price.

1

2

3

4

5

5 1957 CHEVROLET BEL AIR The famous 283ci V-8 with optional fuel injection was introduced in 1957. This was the first American production engine to deliver one horsepower per cubic inch. In fact, the 1960 Rolls-Royce V-8 was based on the Chevy block. **6 & 7 1961 CORVETTE** Mechanically the '61 Corvette was basically unchanged from the previous model, a new, lighter radiator, being the exception. Externally, the new rear-end design was taken from the XP-700 show car. **8 1958 CHEVROLET DEL RAY** All 1958 Chevrolets had the new X-type frame, and were somewhat larger than the previous models. The mid-range Del Ray was powered by a standard 145hp inline 6 or the optional 185hp 283ci V-8.

6

7

8

1 1987 GREENWOOD CORVETTE Over the years a number of aftermarket specialty builders have made their mark working on the Corvette. Best known among them are Reeves Callaway and the two represented here, Greenwood and Eckler (**2 1981 Corvette**). **3 1988 CORVETTE ANNIVERSARY EDITION** Built to celebrate the 35th year of production. **4 1981 CORVETTE STINGRAY. 5 1973 CORVETTE COUPE** In 1973, the year of the 55mph American speed limit, the Corvette was slower than the previous model, but it still could run the quarter-mile in about 15 seconds. **6 1985 CHEVROLET CAMARO IROC-Z** IROC. International Race of Champions: a series in which drivers from different types of racing compete against each other driving identical Chevrolets Camaros. **7 1981 CHEVROLET CAMARO Z-28** The 350ci V-8 was the standard engine, but it only came with automatic transmission. For the performance nut, Chevy would install a 305ci coupled with a manual 4-speed at no extra cost. **8 1987 CORVETTE COUPE** Dollar for dollar the current generation of Corvettes are the best buy in the high-stakes, high-performance marketplace.

1

2

3

1 1974 DE TOMASO PANTERA Designed by Tom Tjaarda for Alejandro De Tomaso in 1969/70, the car is still in production. The first Pantera was a sleekly styled, mid-engine beauty with plenty of stick. In 1970 de Tomaso and Lee Iacocca (then of Ford) made a deal and 1971 found Panteras growling in American Lincoln-Mercury dealerships. The car was hot, but relations between Iacocca and de Tomaso were growing decidedly cold. In 1974 they parted company and there were no U.S.-spec Panteras available until the early 1980's. Subsequent models like the '78 (2) and '83 GT5 (3) have managed to keep up with other exotics in terms of performance. **4 1982 DELOREAN** The final chapter in the DeLorean saga still is being written in various British and American courtrooms, but the car, the DeLorean DMC-12,   4 is no more. An interesting-looking car, it broke no new technical ground. As a performance car it left a lot to be desired, as it was outperformed easily by a host of competitors, including the Corvette, Porsche 944 and Mazda RX-7. **5 1934 DODGE CONVERTIBLE** For 1934, Dodge had a new 217ci 6-cyl. engine and "floating cushion wheels" suspension. Dodge and Chrysler shared chassis and body shells that year, and when the radical Chrysler airflow turned out to be a massive flop, it was the Dodge-bodied Chryslers that averted total disaster. **6 1971 DODGE CHARGER R/T** The first Chargers arrived on the scene in 1966 and almost immediately became one of the most sought-after muscle cars in America. The '71 models, like the R/T seen here, sported new

5

bodywork. The top-of-the-line R/T was available with the standard Hemi or 440ci Magnum V-8. **7 1959 DODGE CUSTOM ROYAL** The Custom Royal was the best Dodge that money could buy, and over 21,000 people bought them. With a 345hp V-8 and optional fuel injection, the Royal was a bargain at its slightly over $3,000 price tag. **8 1970 DODGE SUPERBEE** With its heavy-duty brakes, 3-speed floorshift and big V-8 iron, the Superbee was aimed directly at the young male street racer. The example pictured here is painted in the optional "Hemi orange" color scheme, and has a Charger Daytona wing high above the rear deck.

6

7

8

48 – 1 through 6 THE DUESENBERG MODEL J The Duesenberg Model J was the only American car of its time that was equal to (certainly) or better than (probably) any other car in the world. Introduced on December 1, 1928, 480 Model J's were built before the Maharaja of Indore bought the last one in 1935. What made these cars so great? Everything. A massive, 4 foot-long straight-eight, 32 valve engine with chain-driven double overhead cams, and aluminium rods and pistons that produced 265hp at 4250rpm. Giant 15-inch diameter vacuum boosted brakes. A revolutionary lubrication system that automatically oiled the chassis every 75 miles. Etc., etc. The J could reach 100mph from a standing start in 21 seconds, then continue on into the 115 mph area. Pictured here are a 1930 tourer (**1**), 1929 convertible coupe (**2**) and a 1930 with Rollston coachwork (**3**). The fourth (**4**) is a 1933 supercharged SJ Roadster with coachwork by Walton. If the 'J' was fast the 'SJ' was awesome: 104 mph in second gear; 140 mph in top. This, with a car whose chassis alone weighed over two tons. Approximately 36 SJ's were built between May 1932 and October 1935. The 1935 Duesenberg SJ Speedster pictured here (**5**) is said to have been owned by Clark Gable. Well, if he didn't own it he probably wished he did. The other Duesenberg pictured (**6**) is a 1933 dual-cowl Phaeton by LeBaron.

5

6

1

2

3

4

5

1 1924 DELAGE CO BOATTAIL BY LABOURDETTE
Founded in 1905 by Louis Delage, the firm expanded rapidly, and by 1912 he was selling 1,000 cars per year. Many famous coachbuilders did some of their best work on the Delage chassis. The example shown here features custom coachwork by Henri Labourdette. A dual cowl skiff Phaeton, it is similar to other Labourdette bodies of the time. **2 1911 DELAGE TYPE X** This 1911 Delage Type X won the prestigious Coupe de L'Auto at Boulogne. **5 1938 Delage D8** The 1938 D8, with Le Tourneur et Marchand coachwork, was one of the most beautiful cars of the period. But the Delage was no longer being manufactured by Delage. Business reverses had forced the sale of the company to Delahaye, who kept the nameplate alive until the early '50's. **3 1897 DAIMLER WAGONETTE** The initial year of production for Daimler of Coventry was 1897. With a 2-cyl. engine that developed all of 4hp, one of these cars drove from Scotland to Lands End in England (929 miles) at an average speed of nearly 10mph. **4 1934 DAIMLER 15 DROPHEAD COUPE** This car is typical of the Daimler line in the mid 1930's. Powered by a 6-cyl. ohv 1.8 litre, it was built in response to the

6

7

increasing demand by consumers for smaller, lighter cars. **6 1909 DELAUNAY-BELLEVILLE MODEL 1A-6** Delaunay-Belleville was one of the prestige carmakers in pre-World War I France. Although the firm never regained its popularity after the war, it continued to produce cars until 1950. **7 through 9 DELAHAYE** Although Delahaye began producing cars in 1894, it wasn't until the mid 1930's that they began making the cars that we associate with the name today. In 1934 the newly introduced Type 135 set a number of world speed records at Montlhéry Autodrome. Until the outbreak of World War II, Delahayes like the '38 convertible coupe shown here (**7**), were cloaked in bodies by most of the top European coachbuilders. The first cars built after the war continued to use the prewar 6-cyl. 160hp Type 135 engine and chassis. A fine example with coachwork by Vanden Plas is shown here (**8**). The last Delahaye, the Type 235, had an uprated 135 engine and, again, elegant coachwork by Philippe Charbonneaux (**9**).

8

9

1

2

3

4

1, 2, 3 & 4 EXCALIBER Famed industrial designer Brooks Stevens maintained a lifelong love affair with the classic Mercedes SSK Roadster of the 1920's. In 1964 he formed the Excaliber Company to produce modern versions of his dream car in Milwaukee, Wisconsin. The early cars, like the 1976 Series 3 (**2 & 3**), utilized components from 250 outside manufacturers, including General Motors, which supplied Chevrolet Corvette engines. Between 1975 and 1979, 1,842 of the Series 3 were produced. The 1981 Series 4 (**1**) and the current Series 5 (**4**) employ GM drive trains and running gear, GM 5.7 litre, fuel-injected V-8, and something quite unusual for a specialty carmaker: a warranty that allows owners to have their cars serviced by GM. These handcrafted machines have evolved from the early SSK lookalikes to automobiles with a style that is uniquely their own. No matter what your opinion of their "look," the Excaliber is one of the few real success stories in recent automotive history.

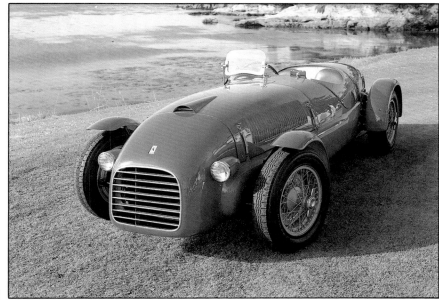

5

6

5 1957 FERRARI 500 MONDIALE The 500 Mondiale sports car was built around the Aurelio Lampredi designed 4-cyl., Formula Two engine, which powered Alberto Ascari to the World Championship in 1952 and 1953. **6 1947 FERRARI 166** The year 1947 marked the appearance of the first Ferrari automobile, the Tipo 125. Naturally, it was powered by a V-12. It didn't finish its first race, but did win the second. This car was superseded Tipo 166 (166cc per cylinder), a cycle fendered, two- seat Spyder Corsa. After winning its first race it was sold to a wealthy sportsman, thus gaining the honor of being the first Ferrari ever sold. **7 1950 FERRARI 212 MILLE MIGLIA** This car is typical of Ferraris during the early '50's. The Superleggera (very light) body by Carrozzeria Touring was made of aluminium, hand formed over a wooden mold. The body was then fastened to the car's tubular steel frame by rolling the edges of the panels around the tubing. **8 1952 FERRARI 340 MEXICO** Three Berlinetta Mexicos were built to compete in the 1952 Carrera Panamericana in Mexico.

7

8

1 1965 FERRARI 275 GTS Introduced in 1965, the Pininfarina bodied car was derived from the 330 GT 2+2. It had a reputation for being somewhat unpredictable in wet conditions. **2 1966 FERRARI DINO 206S** Enzo Ferrari's 24 year old son, Dino, died in 1956. The Dino was created as his memorial. In 1965 the first Dino car, the 260 SP, won the European Hillclimb Championship. **3 1964 FERRARI 330 GT 2+2** Built on a stretched 250 wheelbase, this Pininfarina design received so much criticism for its four headlights that they were dropped in mid 1965. **4 1956 FERRARI 410 SUPERAMERICA** The 410 was Ferrari's attempt to capture a segment of the American luxury, high-performance marketplace. **5 1964 FERRARI 250 LM** This car was designed to replace the GTO in the GT racing category. **6 1968 FERRARI 275 GTB/4** This was the first 4-cam V-12 Ferrari not built specifically for racing. (Although with 300hp at 8000rpm and a 166mph top speed, who could tell?)

1

2

3

4

1

2

3

4

1 1965 FERRARI 330 GT 2+2 Introduced in 1964, the 330 GT 2+2 remained in production through 1967. **2 1972 FERRARI DINO 246 GT** Based on the Pininfarina-designed Dino 206 GT, the 246 GT featured a larger, 2.4-litre engine. In 1973 this model was replaced by the Targa-type Spyder 246 GTS, which was produced through 1974. **3 1978 FERRARI 308 GTS** Designed by Pininfarina, this was the first Ferrari with a fiberglass-reinforced body. It was also one of the first cars to utilize the designer's new wind tunnel. **4 1967 FERRARI 275 GTB/4** Only 350 were made, and they are much sought after today, fetching as much as one million dollars per car. **5 1967 FERRARI 330 P4** If you thought the 275 GTB/4 was expensive, you'd better redefine the term. Only 3 of these 4 litre V-12's exist, and you'll have to come up with at least nine million dollars to park one in your garage. A refinement of the 1966 P3, the P4 body was made by Cigario. This particular car won the Daytona 24 Hour Race and was third at Le Mans. **6 1965 FERRARI 330 GT 2+2** Yet another 330 GT with those &£!*? headlights! **7 1973 FERRARI 365 GTB/4 DAYTONA** The 1968 Pininfarina designed V-12 Daytona was built until 1974, and is considered by many to be the last "real" Ferrari.
OVERLEAF: 1987 FERRARI TESTA ROSSA

5

6

1 1978 FERRARI BERLINETTA BOXER The first Berlinetta Boxer, the 4.4-litre 365 GT/BB appeared in 1973. It was replaced in 1976 by the 4.9 litre 512 BB. **2 1970 FERRARI 512 M** Twenty five of these racers were built in 1969/70. Each was powered by a 4993cc, 550hp V-12. **3 1981 FERRARI 400** A Ferrari with automatic transmission? This was the ideal car for people who wanted to own a Ferrari but didn't really want to own a Ferrari. Introduced in 1976, the 400 was discontinued in 1985. **1985 FERRARI TESTAROSSA** This second generation redhead is dramatic to look at, listen to and drive. It'll get to 60 in less time than it took you to read this caption. **5 1973 FERRARI DINO** A beautiful example of the Targa-type Dino Spyder. **6 FERRARI TESTAROSSA CONVERTIBLE** You say Ferrari doesn't make a convertible. You're right. But what do you want for $142,000? A number of aftermarket specialists will chop your top. Just add another $25,000 to the sticker price. **OVERLEAF: 1985 FERRARI GTO.**

1

2

3

4

1 1985 FERRARI TESTAROSSA Another view of the aerodynamically styled 1985 Testarossa. Its 4 cam aluminium 5- litre flat 12 with 48 valves and 380 horses will move you along life's highway at 181mph. 2 1985 FERRARI 288 GTO GTO. The letters are magic to all Ferraristi. The first GTO, the 250, was introduced in 1962. The 'O' in GTO stands for 'omologato' or, as previously noted, "homologation." The new 288 GTO appeared in 1984. This time the 'O' was needed to qualify the car for international Group B rallying. Put a 393hp, twin-turbo dohc quad V-8 into a 2,555-lb car and you've got 0 to 60 in 5 seconds and a 190mph top speed. Only 272 were built before production stopped in 1986. 3 A 1981 vintage Ferrari 512 BB. 4 "Holy aerofoils, B.A.T. man, a Boxer with wings!" 5Another Testarossa, this one an '87. OVERLEAF: 1988 FERRARI F40 The F-40 was produced to celebrate Ferrari's fortieth year. Even sitting still it looks fast, and it is: 200 mph fast. Forza!

1

2

3

4

1 1951 FORD CRESTLINER Only a few sheet-metal changes differentiated this car from the 1950 model. It did, however, offer the new, optional Ford-O-Matic two-speed transmission for an extra $159. **2 1969 FORD SHELBY MUSTANG GT-350** Created by Le Mans-winning race car driver, Carroll Shelby, the Shelby Mustangs were developed for S.C.C.A. racing (yep, they had to be homologated). They won their class championship in '65, '66 and '67. And the Trans-Am title in '66 and '67. By 1969 Shelby no longer was associated with the cars, and the Mustangs had become more Ford than Shelby. Naturally, sales dropped off and by 1970 the model was discontinued. **3 FORD MODEL A PHAETON 4 1930 MODEL A ROADSTER** Produced under the supervision of Henry Ford's son Edsel, the Model A went into production in November 1927. Its 3.4-litre, 4-cyl. engine provided 40hp and a top speed of 70mph. Within two years over two million had been sold, and by the time it went out of production in 1931 sales had topped five million. **5 1969 FORD MUSTANG PLAYBOY SPECIAL** This particular model was fitted with a rumble seat, of all things.

5

6 1969 MUSTANG MACH 1 The rear airscoops were fakes, but the 250hp, 351ci V-8 certainly was real. **7 1968 FORD SHELBY MUSTANG GT 500 KR** This replacement for the GT 500 had a 428ci, 400hp V-8 to help the King of the Road keep its title. **8 FORD SKYLINER** Finally, a hard-top convertible that actually converted. Ford introduced this unusual retractable-top vehicle in 1957. It worked without a hitch, but sales were disappointing and it was dropped at the end of '59. **9 1957 FORD THUNDERBIRD** The face-lifted '57 T-Bird definitely was bigger than its predecessors, but was it better? Most think not. The only real performance option available was a Paxton centrifugal blower with special cylinder heads that pushed the power up to 340hp at 5300rpm. The sales success of the standard '57 meant that future T-Birds would continue to grow in size as their performance shrunk.

6

7

8

9

1 1978 FORD MUSTANG KING COBRA Called by many the ultimate Mustang, only 500 of these wild looking 302ci V-8 creations were built.
2 FORD MUSTANG "SPORTS ROOF" Positioned just below the Mach 1, the "Sports Roof" was available with a powerful 351ci, 335hp four-barrel V-8. **3 1970 FORD MUSTANG BOSS 302** Another homologation special, the Boss 302 was intended as competition for the Camaro Z-28, in the Trans Am series. It had a special, high output 300hp V-8, with a Holley four-barrel carb and special pistons that pulled the car through the quarter-mile in 14.09 seconds. **4 1971 FORD MUSTANG MACH 1** The restyled Mach 1 was available with an optional 429ci, 400hp V-8.
5 1973 FORD MUSTANG CONVERTIBLE Word had gotten around that '73 would be the last year for the convertible, thereby doubling sales from the previous year. This was also the last of the "big" Mustangs, and is becoming a sought after collectible.

6 1988 FORD RS 200 Created by famed designer Tony Southgate in 1983, the RS 200 was essentially a chopped Sierra. Homologated as a replacement for the Escorts in Group B rallying, it was involved in the fatal accident in Portugal which resulted in the banning of all Group B supercars. **7 1987 FORD MUSTANG GT** The GT, with its front engine, rear drive and live rear axel basically was an old design cloaked in trick new bodywork. But the 5-litre V-8 does go when you put your foot on it. **8 1987 FORD THUNDERBIRD TURBO** The performance car hoped for by the T-Bird faithful in 1955 finally arrived with the 5-litre ohv V-8 '87 Turbo. The SVO option package formerly available on Mustangs is now a T-Bird exclusive, and makes the car a world-class grand tourer. **9 1987 FORD SIERRA RS 500 COSWORTH** The RS 500 is a worldbeater on and off the track. Powered by a Cosworth-designed, aluminium alloy twin-cam 16 valve, fitted with a Garrett-AirResearch blower, the RS 500 will motivate your motoring.

6

7

8

9

1 1913 FIAT TIPO ZERO The Tipo Zero, launched in 1912, was FIAT's first mass-produced model. This 1846cc car reflected FIAT's guiding principle that the future of motoring was not just in sporting models for the privileged racing enthusiast, but in popular, utilitarian vehicles offering sound and affordable engineering and design. **2 1935 FIAT BALLILA** Introduced in 1932, the Tipo 508 Ballila took its name from a Facist youth organization. It offered a 995cc ohv 4-cyl. engine that developed 25hp in touring form and 36hp in its rare, but very desirable racing form. **3 1904 FIAT TOURER** Fabbrica Italiana Automobili Torino, or FIAT, was founded in Turin in 1899, and represented the collaboration of a uniquely talented group of engineers, mechanics and coachbuilders. **4 1967 FIAT DINO** In a rather unusual occurrence, both FIAT and Ferrari debuted a new Dino at the Turin show in 1966. The FIAT Dino was a front engine, rear drive, powered by a 2-litre 160hp V-6. The car would remain in production for six years, but, until recently, was almost ignored by collectors.

5

6

7

5 FRAZER-NASH TT REPLICA The TT (or Tourist Trophy) replica, like all Frazer-Nash models, had a multiple chain transmission instead of a conventional gearbox. The outside shaftlever operated dog clutches on a countershaft in order to send engine power to the desired pair of sprockets. Somehow all this managed to work well enough for the car to win races and influence many people of the British persuasion.
6 1905 FRANKLIN The Franklin was quite unusual, in that it was air, rather than water cooled. Franklin would remain one of the few adherents to air cooling throughout its history (1902-1934).
7 1927 FRAZER-NASH Another member of the chain gang. The last of these chain-driven cars was produced in 1939. The company went out of business in 1960. **8 1948 FRAZER** It was powered by a 3703cc "supersonic" six, and had "torsionectric" suspension. Whatever those were, they weren't enough, and by 1952 the Frazer was gone.

8

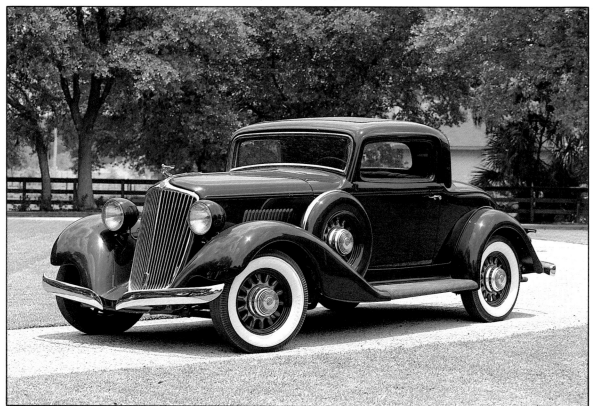

1 1921 HCS Harry Clayton Stutz (HCS) is best remembered for the Stutz Blackhawks and Bearcats he manufactured in the 'teens and 'twenties. After selling the Stutz Company, he began producing another car, the HCS, in 1920. The HCS was a serviceable car but not up to par with his Stutz automobiles, and ceased production in 1923. **2 1941 GRAHAM HOLLYWOOD** The Graham brothers had begun producing cars under the Graham-Paige name in 1928. They were highly thought of in Europe, where a model 619 won the 1929 Monte Carlo Rally. The 822 shown here (**4**) is a good example of the marque. By 1933, when the Custom Eight coupe was introduced (**3**) they were being advertised as "the most imitated car on the road." In 1937 they decided to do some imitating of their own and bought the Cord manufacturing dies from the receivers of the bankrupt Auburn Corp., and set about designing a new Cord-based car, the Graham Hollywood. Introduced in 1940, it had a blown 140hp engine and unit body construction. The car was well received, but production problems and a shortage of cash doomed the company after less than two years.

5 HEALEY TICKFORD
The two-door, 4-litre, four-seat sports saloon with Tickford coachwork had one of the most successful production runs of all the Healey models. The first of these were built upon "C"-type chassis, and in 1951 the "BT" and "F"-types were introduced. In all, 241 were built.
6 1952 HENRY J One of the first American compacts, the Henry J (named for its builder, Henry J. Kaiser) also was available under the Allstate nameplate. After an initial surge sales dwindled, and by the end of 1954 both cars had ceased production. **7 1935 HILLMAN MINX** William Hillman was known primarily for producing reliable, if uninteresting, cars. The 118cc Minx, introduced in 1932, was the most famous of the marque. A sportier version, the Aero Minx (**9**) was added in 1933. Hillman ceased production in 1976. **8 1947 HEALEY ELLIOT** Built by Donald Healey, this sedan and its covertible counterpart, the Westland, were undistinguished. Fortunately for his reputation, he also was responsible for the Nash- Healey and the Austin-Healey.

1

2

3

1– 6 HISPANO-SUIZA Designed by a Swiss, Marc Birkigt, and made in Barcelona and Paris, these are among the most sought-after cars in the world. Pre-World War I models were innovative and fast, winning many races between 1910 and 1915. Cars manufactured prior to 1919 (**3**) took a backseat to the production of aircraft engines for the Allied cause. At war's end, production began on the H-6. This remarkable car, which remained in production until 1931, had a 90-lb. camshaft, which was milled from a solid 700-lb., forged steel billet. The 1924 example pictured here (**5**), with its distinctive tulipwood body by Nieuport, is one of the best known of the marque. The H-6 was replaced by the Type 68, the most famous of all Hispano-Suizas. The Sauotchik-bodied 1934 68 bis convertible shown here (**4**) had an 11-litre V-12 engine and could reach 110 mph. Two other V-12 examples are shown: A 1933 68 bis Cabriolet by Van Vooren (**2**), and a 1938 CABRIOLET (**6**). The 1937 K-6 (**1**) had a 5184cc straight six. Hispano-Suiza ended production in 1939. **OVERLEAF: HISPANO-SUIZA H-6B BOATTAIL**

4

5

1 **1911 HUPMOBILE MODEL 20 RUNABOUT** The Model 20 commenced production in 1909 and ended two years later. This car, painted "Hupmobile Blue," is one of four models produced that year. Hupmobiles remained in production until 1940. **2, 6 & 8 HUDSON** The Terraplane was considered one of the hot cars of the 'thirties. The 1937 model pictured here (**2**) was one of the last Terraplanes, as Hudson decided to drop the model name. The 1950 Commodore Eight (**8**) featured a new "step-down" chassis and the old reliable Hudson straight eight powerplant. The 308ci, 145hp L-head, 6-cyl. Hudson Hornet (**6**) appeared in 1951 and was NASCAR champion in '52 and '53. **3 1932 HORCH V-12** Built by August Horch, these luxury touring cars had 6021cc 120hp V-12 engines and ZF transmissions. **4 1904 HUMBERETTE** The Humberette had a single-cylinder 5hp engine and tubular chassis. **5 1950 HOTCHKISS** Winner of the first postwar Monte Carlo Rally in 1949. **7 1933 ISOTTA FRASCHINI TIPO 8A** After the First World War Isotta Fraschini began building large, luxury touring cars like this Phaeton with Castanga coachwork.

1

2

JAGUAR William Lyons, founder of the Jaguar firm, began by manufacturing special coachwork under the Swallow name. He was to continue to dominate the company for several decades, seeing it through several changes of emphasis and style, although the basic aims of "Grace, Pace and Space" remained the watchwords of this extraordinary engineer. The popularity of the Swallow SS (Standard Saloon) series prompted Lyons to begin building the entire car under a new name: Jaguar. The unfortunate fact that the Swallow SS shared its initials with Hitler's elite military unit, the SS also helped to make the new Jaguar name more acceptable to the post-war British buying public than the old pre-war name. The 2.5-litre ohv SS 100 (the 100 stood for its top speed) remained in production until the outbreak of war in 1939. (**1 & 2**) The first postwar cars, like the 1946 Saloon shown here (**3**), were but a lead-in to one of the most exciting sports cars of all time, the **XK 120** (**5**). Introduced in 1948, it had the first pure Jaguar engine. This 3442cc inline 6cyl. produced 160hp and moved the car along at 120mph. The model that replaced it, the **XK 140** (**4**), offered improved steering and a 210hp engine. It would remain in production through 1956.

3

4

5

6

7

8

(6) **1937 JAGUAR SS DROPHEAD** This 1.5 litre had a new-style radiator grille nestled between the oversized Lucas headlights. (7) **1958 JAGUAR MK IX** The Mark IX had a new 3.8 litre XK engine, four wheel disc brakes and could reach 114mph. (8) **1954 JAGUAR XK 140** (9) **1959 JAGUAR XK 150** The XK 140 was uprated in 1957, receiving a new designation, the XK 150. Larger, heavier and more powerful, it was much more comfortable than its predecessors. Many purists argue that the increase in size and comfort rather spoilt the startlingly elegant lines of the original 120, which had so enthralled the motoring public when it first appeared in a post-war world more used to austerity and rationing than to the outspoken sleekness and speed of the new Jaguar range.

9

1 Introduced in 1961, the E-Type was unequaled in its combination of style and performance. Monocoque construction, independent rear suspension, wire wheels, disc brakes and a 3.8 litre engine moved the sleek cat from 0 to 60 in 6.8 sec. and topped out at 150mph. 3 The roadster version was equally beautiful. Probably the most significant change to the E-Type was the addition of a V-12 in 1971. The 5343cc dohc engine developed 325hp, and would remain the E-Type powerplant until the end of its production run in 1975. 2 The XJ-6, which was introduced in 1968, is a high performance touring car capable of speeds in excess of 120mph. A V-12 powerplant was added in 1972. 6 The XJS replaced the 2+2 E-Type in 1975. A true GT car, the XJS would reach an honest 155mph. Still in production, it has evolved over the years with various detail refinements. 5 Pictured here is the 1985 Golden Jubilee Model XJS HE with coachwork by Guy Salmon.
OVERLEAF: JAGUAR E-TYPE

1

2

3

4

5

1,2 & 4 1987 JAGUAR XJ-S CONVERTIBLE This model is powered by a 5.3 litre V-12 that develops 262 hp at 5000rpm. With special cylinder heads and other improvements made by Swiss engineer, Michael May, this engine is able to combine fuel efficiency with an 11 to 1 compression ratio. The convertible model combines the speed and comfort of the more usual saloon with the sheer exhilaration of wind-in-the-hair motoring, which some Jaguar enthusiasts feared had gone for good only a few years before this model made its appearance. **3 1988 SOVEREIGN** This vehicle is produced under the name of Jaguar's sister company Daimler, and is the latest version of this luxury touring sedan. **5 1963 JENSEN MARK III C-V8** Founded by the Jensen brothers in 1936, the firm was known for fast, stylish GT cars. The '63 C-V8 was powered by a 5.9 litre Chrysler V-8 with Torque Flight automatic transmission. **6 & 7 JENSEN INTERCEPTOR** Introduced in 1968, the Interceptor was the last model made under the Jensen name. Powered by an even larger engine, a Chrysler 6.3 litre V-8, the two ton car was capable of 125 mph.

1 **1984 KVA FORD GT-40 REPLICA** The GT-40 was one of the most awesome racing cars ever to traverse the Mulsanne straight. Of the 100 produced, about 30 were intended for use on the highway. The GT-40 won Le Mans in 1966, '67 and '68. The demand for the car far exceeds the supply, so specialty firms like KVA build identical-looking fiberglass replicas to satisfy the fantasy. **2, 3, 4, 5 & 6 LAGONDA** Lagonda had been making cars for 26 years prior to this 1932 2-litre, low chassis Speed Model (2). The 1937 LG.45 Town Car (3) is one example of the many LG.45's produced by Lagonda after it changed ownership in 1935. LG.45's were luxury touring cars that exceeded 100mph. The 4.5-litre, 135hp engine from the earlier M.45 Rapide (5) was, with periodic updates, the powerplant of all LG.45 models. The V-12 Lagondas made their debut in 1937. The example shown here (6) is a 2/4 passenger roadster built to special order by Gurney Nutting for the Maharajah of Indore.

3

4

5

6

1

2

1 to 5 LAMBORGHINI COUNTACH The ultimate dream machine of the modern era. Considered by many the most super of supercars: the Lamborghini Countach. It's hard to believe that the Countach debued at the Geneva show in 1971. Of course there have been detail changes over the years, but essentially what you saw in Geneva is what you still get. Not bad either. The powerplant of this magnificent performance car has changed no less than three times over the years. The 1971 prototype featured a 5 litre V-12 engine, but this was altered to a 4 litre engine which was smaller but nonetheless able to push the car to around 174mph. In 1982 the Countach gained a 4754cc engine which was in turn replaced by a 5.2 litre, four valve motor in 1986. **OVERLEAF: LAMBORGHINI COUNTACH**

3

5

6

7

1 1965 LAMBORGHINI 350 GT The first production Lamborghini. Body by Carrozzeria Touring. A quad cam V-12 270hp engine, 150mph top speed and exquisite hand craftmanship set the tone for all future models. The GT 350 was enlarged slightly to become the 400 GT 2+2. **2 A 1975 COUNTACH 3 & 4 LAMBORGHINI SILHOUETTE** The Silhouette's removable roof panels made it the first "open" Lamborghini. Derived from the Urraco, the Silhouette's V-12 put out 255hp and its road holding was superb. Only 52 were made between 1976 and 1979. **5 & 7 LAMBORGHINI JALPA** As is obvious from the photos, the Jalpa evolved from the Silhouette. The Jalpa debuted in 1982 and is still in production. Its 3.5-litre, 255hp V-8 will move it to 150+ mph. **6 & 8 1988 COUNTACH** 1988 was Lamborghini's 25th. anniversary. The 5000 Quattrovalvole V-12 powering this car (**6**) is a 5.2 litre 455hp screamer that tops out at 173mph and still meets U.S. emission standards. **8** The LP 500 is slightly less exotic but not enough to bother most people.

8

The startlingly sleek and graceful **LAMBORGHINI COUNTACH** is the latest product of the Italian business magnate Ferruccio Lamborghini. Having made a fortune from air-conditioning and farm machinery, Lamborghini acquired a Ferrari but was unimpressed by its modest comforts and Enzo Ferrari's attitude. He therefore decided to produce a better car than the Ferrari, no mean ambition. He succeeded brilliantly with the Miura in 1966 and with the Countach in 1974. The latter is said to have acquired its name when Lamborghini's production staff first saw the design and remarked 'countach', a barely printable exclamation of admiration in the local vernacular.

1

2

3

4

5

6

7

1 1929 LINCOLN MODEL L DUAL COWL PHAETON Forty two of these dual-cowl phaetons were produced in 1929. **2 1957 LINCOLN PREMIER** The '57 Premier was similar to the '56, which won an award from the Industrial Designers Institute for excellence in automotive design. **3 - 7 LINCOLN CONTINENTAL** The first Continental, which was made as a one-off for Edsel Ford, was acclaimed at the time as the most beautiful car ever designed. Subsequent production models in '40 and '41 (**4 and 6**) showed their striking Lincoln Zephyr-based, Eugene Gregorie design to be a winner with American car buyers. Production was halted by the war in 1942 and would not be resumed until 1946. At the end of the '48 model year the car, though still in demand, was dropped. **5** The Continental was brought back in 1956 as the Mark II. **3** The Mark V, while adequate in luxury terms, was far from classic. The more current versions, however, are top-quality grand touring cars typified by this Mark VII (**7**).

1 1971 LOTUS EUROPA This small, mid-engine car was powered by the standard 1470cc four, or the uprated 1558cc, 126hp dohc used in the Elan Sprint. **2 1962 LOTUS ELITE** 1,030 Elites were produced between 1958 and 1967. This car established Lotus, and Colin Chapman, as important car constructors. This "road-going racer" was sold at a loss of about 100 per car. Lessons learned on the Elite would be put to use with the profitable Elan. **3 1971 LOTUS ELAN +2 S130** The +2 version was introduced in 1967. It had a five-speed gearbox and the 126hp Sprint engine. **4 1989 LOTUS EXCEL** The 2+2 Excel is capable of 0 to 60 in 7.2 seconds and a top speed of 130mph. **5 1989 LOTUS ESPRIT TURBO** We're talking supercar here. A serious car for serious drivers. First produced in 1975, the Esprit was uprated with the addition of a turbocharger in 1983 and styling refinements for '88. Performance is what this car's about: 0 to 60 in 5.2 seconds and a top speed of 156mph.

1

2

3

4

1 **1931 MARMON 141 CONVERTIBLE SEDAN**
Designed and built by Herman Marmon from 1902 to 1933, Marmons were big, fast and beautifully made. Various models had straight 8's, V-8's and, like the Model 141, V-16 power.
2 **1949 MASERATI COUPE** Maserati, like Alfa Romeo and Ferrari, has a strong racing heritage dating from the 1930's. The postwar years saw racing greats like Fangio, Moss and Behra drive for the marque. Maserati road cars of this period, while not made in quantity, were, as can be seen here, quite beautiful. 3, 4 & 5 **1980 MASERATI MERAK SS** A smaller version of the Bora, the Merak was powered by the V-6 engine designed for the Citroën SM. The Merak also utilized some of the SM's sophisticated hydraulics. The Merak SS was lighter and had a more powerful 220hp engine. 6 **1987 MAZDA RX-7 TURBO** As the only succesful manufacturer of rotary- engined cars, Mazda is one of the true automotive originals.

1

2

3

4

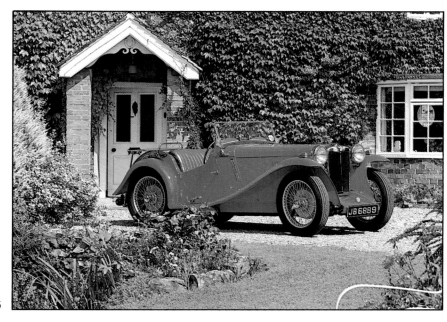

5

6

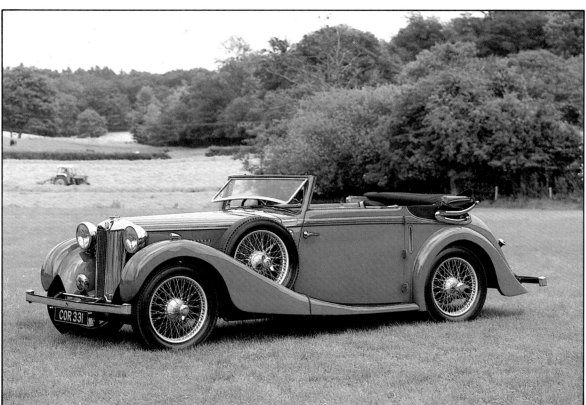

8

7

9

MG The first MG's (for Morris Garages) appeared sometime in 1923 or 1924, and for the next 25 years produced a bewildering array of models rivaling only Mercedes in the use of confusing nomenclature. Herewith a gaggle of MG's from the mid-1930's: The first modern MG was the 1932 J2 Midget. It is the "father" of all MG's right up to the TF of the mid-50's (**4**). The 1934 N Magnette with its 1286cc, 6-cyl. KD type engine, coupled with light weight and quick handling, was formidable on tight, twisty roads. The immortal Tazio Nuvolari won the 1933 Tourist Trophy race in a supercharged K-3 Magnette. The 1935 PA (**5**) had a 750cc engine while the 1936 PB series cars (**1, 2 & 8**), with 939cc and 43hp, offered a bit more in the way of performance. The two more elegant VA series cars, the 1938 (**3**) and the Tickford-bodied 1937 (**7**) had 1548cc engines based on the Wolesley Twelve. Tickford also was responsible for the 1936 SA coupe(**9**). The SA's represented a shift by management away from racing oriented sports cars to saloons like this 1936 example (**10**). The 1937 Midget TA (**6**) was built on a larger chassis, giving it a roomier passenger compartment. Its 50hp engine gave it performance equal to the smaller models

10

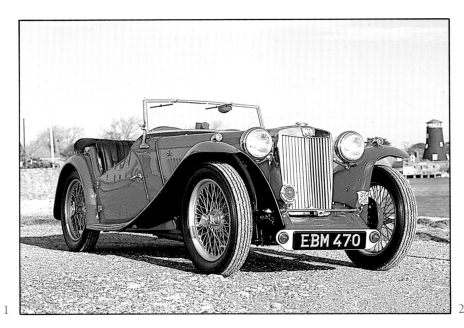

1

2

4

3

5

2 1938 MG WA In August 1938 the Tickford-bodied drophead coupe joined the MG lineup. This was still larger and more powerful than earlier models. The car was uprated in 1939 but by then war was at hand and no new MG's would be built until 1945. **1 & 7 MG TC** It may have looked and acted like the prewar models, but it was the TC that caught the imagination of the young, postwar generation. It had a 1250cc, 4-cyl. pushrod engine that delivered two things: 54hp, and more importantly, fun. The TC and it's progeny, the TD and TF (**8**), along with the Jag XK 120, made "sports car" a household term in the United States. The classic era came to an end in 1955 with the introduction of the MG A, which remained in production until 1962. **6** Seen here is a 1622cc MK 2 roadster. Late in 1962 the A gave way to the B (**5**), which would continue until 1980, becoming the best-selling of all MG's. **4** The 6-cyl. Model C of 1967-69 delivered 145hp and a top speed of 120mph. **3** The 1980 MG Midget was powered by the 1500cc Triumph Spitfire engine. Though it sold in excess of 225,000 it wasn't enough, and in 1980 the factory was closed.

6

1 **1907 METALLURGIQUE** Made in Belgium from 1898 to 1927, the Metallurgique had a pressed steel chassis. A 10 litre engine was standard in 1907. **2 1948 MORGAN 4/4** Beginning with the first three-wheelers in the early 1900's, Morgan has always done it their way. The Plus Four and its derivative, the Plus Eight, continue to be in limited production and still use some of the original design features of the pre-World War II models. A nice car, the Morgan. **3 1922 MERCER** Mercer, which only lasted for 15 years, had an enviable record on the racetracks of America, particularly in the hands of Barney Oldfield. **4 1929 MOON** Made by Scottish-born Joseph Moon, the cars are easily identified by their imitation Rolls-Royce grilles. This model, the Prince of Windsor, was powered by a 4.4- litre straight 8. **5 1950 MERCURY MONARCH CUSTOM** A wonderful example of a customized '50's leadsled. A "chopped" roofline and sculpted bodywork make this a singular dream machine. **6 1940 MERCURY 8** Mercury began life as a model designation in the Ford line, but

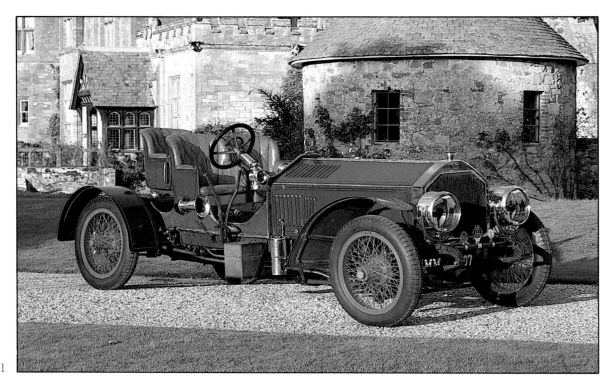

1

2

3

4

in 1940 it gained its own identity as the car positioned between Ford and Lincoln. This convertible shows its Zephyr heritage. **7 1987 MITSUBISHI STARION TURBO** This traditional front-engine, rear-drive car features a 2.6-litre, fuel-injected, intercooled turbo 155hp engine which will move the car at 137mph. **8 1957 MERCURY TURNPIKE CRUISER** The Turnpike Cruiser began life as a show car designed to "give American motorists the maximum driving pleasure, comfort, and safety as they travel the new turnpikes." The large greenhouse was "a salient feature to permit full enjoyment of the wide new vistas opened to turnpike travellers." One new vista was the Indianapolis Motor Speedway, where the Turnpike Cruiser served as pace car in 1957. **9 1947 MERCURY** The first postwar models, like this two door sedan, were undistinguished. It wasn't until 1949 that the marque began to take off.

5

6

7

8

9

1

2

3

4

5

1 - 6 MERCEDES-BENZ The original Mercedes cars were designed by William Maybach and encompassed both racers and touring cars. Known as Mercedes Simplex, the cars pictured here are typical of Maybach's work: **2 1903 Model 28/32** . **3 1904 28/32 HP Phaeton** . **6 1907 28/60 Simplex** and the **1 1907 HP Simplex Sports Wagon**. In 1907 Maybach was succeeded by Paul Daimler. **5 The 1912 "Big Bertha"** is typical of the chain-driven cars of the period. Though Daimler withdrew from racing from 1908 to 1913, it made an historic comeback at the 1914 French Grand Prix, where the 4-cyl., 16- valve 115hp sohc-engined racers (**4**) propelled Mercedes to a triumphant 1, 2, 3, finish.

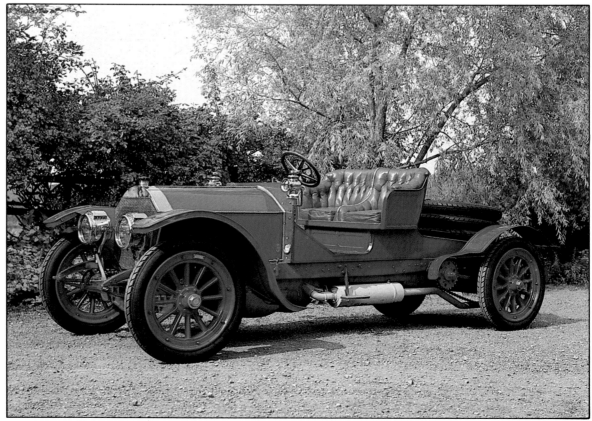

6

7

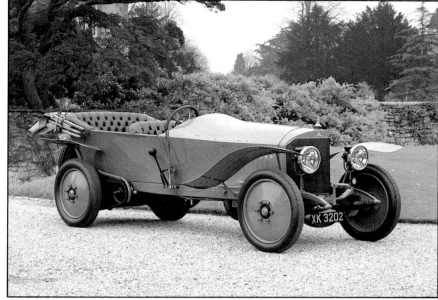

8

7 - 10 MERCEDES-BENZ Prince Henry
of Prussia was an avid sportsman who
sponsored a series of motor "trials" beginning in
1908. Won by a Benz, the event led to the
introduction of a range of sports cars, among
them the 1912 37/90 Prince Henry Torpedo (**8**).
In 1926, newly merged Daimler-Benz unveiled
the Type 24/110/160 designed by Ferdinand
Porsche. Commonly referred to as the K Type, it
had a 6.25-litre, 6cyl. ohv engine that was
capable of 160hp with the supercharger
engaged. Handling and brake problems led to
the development of the Type S. The S had a
larger, 6.8-litre, engine and a lighter chassis.
Seen here: **7 1927 Model K, 9 1927 Model
K Gangloff Tourer, and 10 1928 Model S
36/22. OVERLEAF: 1938 540K SINDLEFINGER
CABRIOLET** Powered by a supercharged 5.4-litre
straight 8 that could reach 60 in 14 seconds and
top out at 105mph, the dramatic 540K was the
ultimate expression of prewar German
automaking.

9

10

1

2

3

MERCEDES-BENZ The new German autobahns, built for high speed, literally paved the way for the 540K's and their smaller counterparts, the 5-litre 500K's. Seen here are **6 the 1935 500K, 1 the 1936 500K Sedanca Drophead and 3 the 1936 540K Cabriolet**. The 1936 Type 200 Saloon was developed from the successful Type 171. It was mechanically advanced featuring hydraulic brakes, central chassis lubrication and swing axel rear suspension. The Type 220 was introduced in 1951, yet reflected pre-war styling influences. Powered by a 2.2 litre 6cyl., its advanced cooling and lubrication systems allowed trouble free high speed cruising. **2** Seen here is a 1953 model. **5 The 1927 36/220 S** shown here is but another example of the 'S' cars discussed on page 113. **OVERLEAF: MERCEDES-BENZ 300SL GULLWING**

4

5

6

1

2

3

4

1 1956 MERCEDES-BENZ 190SL The 190SL was introduced in 1956. Based on the Type 180 sedan, 26,000 190SL's were built between 1956 and 1963. **2, 3, 4 & 5 MERCEDES-BENZ 300SL** The 300SL was the road version of the legendary 300SLR racing car. Featuring a multitube, space-frame chassis and futuristic coupe body with "gullwing" doors, the 300SL was the first production car to come with fuel injection as standard equipment. Capable of 165mph, these cars are among the most sought after collectibles in the world. Pictured here are four examples produced between 1955 and 1957 including the roadster version (2). This convertible version was produced in much smaller numbers than the moe sophisticated gull-wing model and is correspondingly more difficult to find in modern classic car auctions.

1 1965 MERCEDES-BENZ 220 SEC CONVERTIBLE Powered by a 2.2-litre six, 1965 was the last year of production for this popular model. **2 1970 MERCEDES BENZ 600 PULLMAN LIMOUSINE** The name Pullman was adopted in order to foster American acceptance of the model. **3 1987 MERCEDES-BENZ 300SL** The current S-class Mercedes cars are sophisticated, powerful Grand Touring cars that manage to live up to their illustrious heritage. **4 1983 MERCEDES-BENZ 230CE** The CE series was supposed to be aimed at young couples without children or older couples whose children have left home or anyone who wants to move up from the 190's but not all the way up. Or something like that. **5 1986 MERCEDES-BENZ 300 SEL 6 1982 MERCEDES-BENZ 500SL ROADSTER** These cars are fast, quiet and easy to drive. **7 1983 MERCEDES-BENZ 500SEC COUPE** This car weighs 3,945 lbs, has every creature comfort you can imagine to sap its power, yet it can motivate from 0 to 60 in 7 seconds. Nice.

1, 2, 3 & 4 MORRIS Morris was Britain's best-selling make between the wars, led first by the "Bullnose" Cowley and Oxford models, which endured from 1919 to 1926 (**2**). Their most popular engine was a 1548cc, 24hp 4cyl. that could run at about 50mph. Morris dropped the "Bullnose" look after 1926 and began to produce a wider variety of types. **3 The Model Ten** featured pressed steel construction. **1 The Morris Eight**, introduced in 1935, moved the company to top of British sales charts. It featured the same engine as its predecessors, but added hydraulic brakes. **4 Morris Minor** The story goes that Lord Nuffield, who was head of operations at Morris, looked at the prototype Morris Minor and said it looked like a poached egg. No matter, the car stayed in production for 23 years (1948-1971). The 1000 model designation was added in 1957 when engine displacement was increased to 948cc's. The convertible seen here is a '67.

1

2

3

4

5

6

5 1932 NASH SEDAN The 1932 Nash line offered stiff X-type frames and a 322ci, 125hp 8-cyl. engine. **6 1956 NASH AMBASSADOR** Hudson and Nash merged in 1954 to form American Motors with George Romney as its chairman. The Ambassador utilized the Packard 320ci, 208hp engine and Twin Ultramatic transmission. **7 1953 NASH-HEALEY CONVERTIBLE** Built at Donald Healey's works in England from 1950 to 1954, the car used a Nash engine refitted with an aluminium head. It developed 140hp and had a top speed of 110mph. After 1952 the bodies were designed by Pininfarina. Approximately 500 of the cars were made. **8 1933 NASH SPECIAL 8 CONVERTIBLE SEDAN** Although Nash was never known for styling, some beautiful models were turned out including this 1933 convertible.

7

8

1 1911 POPE HARTFORD This American marque lasted only from 1903 to 1914. At the time this 7 passenger tourer was offered, 14 different models were available with either 36 or 44 hp engines. **2 1902 PANHARD-LEVASSOR** This firm was among the largest automotive companies in the world in 1902, turning out about 75 cars per month. Credited with introducing the front engine, rear-drive layout, the firm also won the first Paris-Bordeaux race. **3 1910 OTTO** Made in France from 1901 to 1914. **5 1970 OLDSMOBILE CUTLASS SUPREME** The Cutlass supreme was powered by a 350ci ohv V-8 rated at 310hp. **6 1964 OLDSMOBILE F-85 CONVERTIBLE** The F-85 was Oldsmobile's entry in the pony-car sweepstakes. It didn't win. **7 1970 OLDSMOBILE CUTLASS** This was the 1970 Cutlass Supreme, only less so. **8 1971 OLDSMOBILE 4-4-2** 1971 was the high-performance 4-4-2's last model year. Oldsmobile's muscle car had dual exhausts, heavy duty wheels and bucket seats.

1

2

3

4

1 1934 PACKARD SEVEN-PASSENGER TOURER
"Ask the man who owns one." This slogan certainly fits the many beautiful models produced by Packard in the 1930's, including this stunning V-12 with coachwork by Dietrich. **2 1936 PACKARD 120-B SEDAN** The 120 was introduced in January 1935 and was small for a Packard, weighing only about 3,400 lbs. **3 1936 PACKARD V-12** Packard excellence inspired many of the era's greatest coachbuilders: Dietrich, Rollston and Howard "Dutch" Darrin of Paris, who created this one-off boattail in 1936 on a 135-in. chassis. **4 1938 PACKARD-ROLLSTON DC PHAETON** This example by Rollston is on a 1608 chassis. **5 1933 PACKARD V-12** Packard's V-12 began as a twin-six, obtaining its V-12 designation in the 1933 model year. Refinements included a single dry-plate clutch and a Stromberg carb with an automatic choke. **6 1932 PACKARD CONVERTIBLE** In 1930 Clyde Paton was brought over from Studebaker as chief experimental engineer. He was responsible for the "Ride Control" suspension in 1932. **OVERLEAF: 1934 PACKARD 1105 COUPE ROADSTER** Another example of Dietrich coachwork.

5

6

1 1939 PACKARD 1700 CONVERTIBLE The 1700 series V-12's introduced in September 1938 were identical to the '37 models with minor alterations, such as a new steering column gearshift. **2 1937 PACKARD V-12 CONVERTIBLE** New independent front suspension meant better handling for the 16 series cars of 1937. Sales that year soared to 122,500, up from a low of 4,800 in 1933. **3 1934 PACKARD EIGHT** The big news for the Eight that year was the return of custom cars to the line, with bodies by Dietrich and Le Baron. Although most sales continued to be those of the 1103 model, which was being sold for only $2,350. **4 1920 PACKARD TWIN SIX TOWN CAR** This Twin Six special by Fleetwood was made for the Atwater Kents (of radio fame). **7 1953 PACKARD CARIBBEAN** The Caribbean was a show car that actually made it into production. Standard features, unique at the time, included full leather interior, chrome-plated wire wheels and a fishtail rear fender treatment with a continental tire mounting. **6 1956 PACKARD CLIPPER** In 1955 Packard introduced new bodies with V-8 power and these remained essentially unchanged for 1956. This was to be the last year of production for the "real" Packard, the merger with Studebaker only a holding action against its inevitable demise. **5 1958 PACKARD HAWK** The last car to carry the proud Packard name was actually a Studebaker, albeit one of the better models. Only 588 were built.

1

2

3

PIERCE-ARROW The Pierce Company of Buffalo, New York, debuted its first single-cylinder Motorette in 1901. **2** Another early model was the Great Arrow, which won five consecutive Glidden Tours starting in 1905. The marque was always known for the size of its creations, including the 824ci Great Six in 1907. **3** The Gentleman's Roadster, like other models made until 1920, was a right-hand drive. Pierce-Arrow was popular with a diverse group of customers: A 1917 model was Woodrow Wilson's choice of limousine, while bootleggers in the 'twenties appreciated its silence and dependability. **1** The 1931 coupe displays the characteristic fender- mounted headlamps, standard since 1913. A V-12 was introduced in late 1931 to partner the popular six. In 1928 the company merged with Studebaker and produced a series of magnificent touring phaetons (**4 & 5**) and convertibles like this 1932 model (**6**). Financial difficulties dogged the company after it regained its independence in 1933, and it was ultimately sold at auction on May 13, 1938, a Friday.

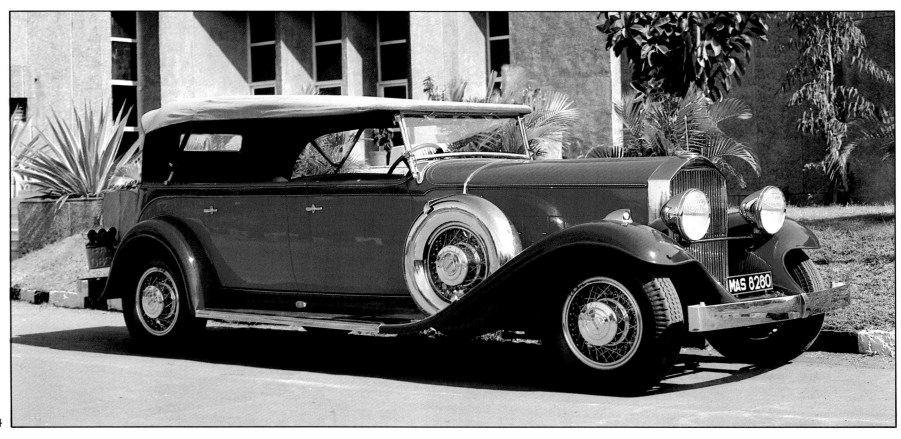

4

5

6

1 1958 PLYMOUTH BELVEDERE This is a classic example of Virgil Exner's "Flight Sweep" styling which first appeared in 1957. The tailfins were gone by 1961. **2, 3, 4 & 6 1970 PLYMOUTH SUPERBIRD** In 1970 the new Superbird lured "King" Richard Petty back to the Plymouth racing stable and the Hemi-powered car took the checker 21 times. Extensive aerodynamic research, carried out by Chrysler's Special Vehicles Group in Lockheed's wind tunnel, resulted in the distinctive, long nose-cone and rear wing. The height of the wing was determined by the need for the trunk to open on the homologated production models. The Superbird and its sister car, the Dodge Daytona, were so dominant that NASCAR modified the rules and did what no other manufacturer could do: beat them. **5 1969 PLYMOUTH GTX 440** The GTX was one of MOPAR's hottest entries into the muscle car field. Powered by the famed Hemi, it could reach 60mph in 6.1 seconds, and turn the quarter in 13.8. **7 1970 PLYMOUTH AAR 'CUDA** This is generally regarded as Chrysler's best performance street car. A 0 to 60 in 5.8 seems to justify the claim. AAR stood for All-American Racers (Dan Gurney's outfit). The engine was a modified 340ci V-8.

3 1937 PONTIAC SEDAN 1937 brought extensive changes to the Pontiac line including a longer, 122-in. wheelbase and a 100hp straight 8 that gave the cars an 85mph top speed. **1 1948 PONTIAC SILVER STREAK** Pontiac's famed Silver Streak styling was originally devised so that the stripes would cover joints in the sheet metal. In 1948 Hydra-Matic transmissions became a popular option. **2 1951 PONTIAC CHIEFTAN DELUXE** In 1951 Pontiac celebrated its silver anniversary. The- top-of-the-line car was powered by a 266.4ci, 116hp straight 8. The engine was placed well forward in the chassis and the back seat mounted ahead of the rear axel, giving passengers a "cradle ride." **4 1956 PONTIAC STARCHIEF** Pontiac had introduced its first V-8 in '55 and more changes came in '56, including a special 285hp engine option.

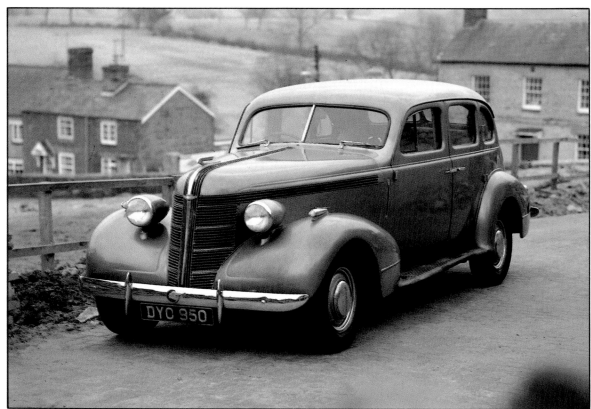

5

6

7

8

9

5 1965 PONTIAC GTO Weighing less than 3,200 lbs, but with 335hp under the hood, the GTO could hit 60 in under 6 seconds. This first "muscle car" was voted by readers of *Car and Driver* magazine, "Best All-Around Car" by a wide margin. **6 1974 PONTIAC TRANS AM 455 SUPER DUTY** Pontiac restyled its Firebird Trans Am line in '74, introducing the shovel-nose, and reducing the power. But, if you felt the need for speed, the 455ci Super Duty V-8 was available as an option and, a rarity for muscle cars, so was the Turbo-HydraMatic transmission. **7 1979 PONTIAC GRAND AM SPORT COUPE** First introduced in 1973, the Grand Am line merged the "luxury of the Grand Prix and the performance and handling of the Trans Am." Right. **8 1988 PONTIAC GRAND PRIX** Your basic GM chassis mated to your basic GM 2.8-litre V-6. Available with 5-speed manual or 4-speed automatic. **9 1979 PONTIAC TRANS AM DAYTONA 500 PACE CAR REPLICA** This is a case where the name just about says it all. **10 1988 PONTIAC BONNEVILLE SSE** This top-of-the-line Bonneville features a 3.8-litre V-6, ABS braking, Y99 Rally Tuned suspension package and electronic, self-leveling ride control.

10

1 1952 PORSCHE 356 Ferdinand Porsche built the first model 356 in Austria, but soon moved the works to its present location in Germany. The 356 offered engines ranging in size from 1086cc to 1966cc. **2 1975 PORSCHE 911 TURBO** Introduced at the Paris show in 1974, the 911 Turbo was planned as a limited production model but, as we all know, it didn't quite work out that way. **3 1965 PORSCHE 911S** At the end of 1964, Porsche debuted a car with the first major design changes in sixteen years: the 911. Among other things, it was the first Porsche production car with a 5- speed transmission. Three decades later, it's still going strong. **4 1959 PORSCHE 365B SPEEDSTER** Introduced in '59, this model was named the "D" convertible because the body was made by Reutter in Drauz. **5 1955 PORSCHE 356 SPEEDSTER** The 356 Speedster first appeared in 1954. It came with a 1500cc engine that delivered 55hp (Standard) or 70hp (Super), with corresponding top speeds of 99.5 and 100.5mph. **6 1958 PORSCHE 356A SUPER 75 COUPE** The year 1958 marked the official end of production for the 356A.

2

3

1 1979 PORSCHE 911SC COUPE Introduced in 1978, the SC was to have been the final 911 model, since its planned replacement, the front-engined 928, already had gone into production. However, public demand kept the 911 alive, and in 1981 the new Porsche chairman, Peter Schutz, confirmed his intention to continue producing the car. **2 1982 PORSCHE 930 TURBO** The term 930 "Turbo" is redundant, according to Porsche. They gave the model designation "Type 930" to the Turbo when it was first developed. So, a 911 Turbo is a model 930 Porsche no matter what you call it. The Turbo "look" became so popular that today the Turbo is offered in three body styles: Coupe, Targa and Cabrio. **3 1977 PORSCHE 911 CARRERA** In 1977 the Carrera went up to 3 litres and 200hp. In 1978 it would be replaced by the 911SC. **OVERLEAF: 1982 PORSCHE 911SC**

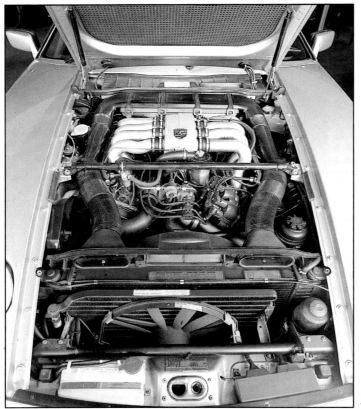

1 **1979 PORSCHE TURBO** The Turbo, introduced as a 1975 model, was unchanged until 1978, when capacity went up to 3299cc and power to 300hp. 2 **1986 DP MOTORSPORTS 911 CONVERSION** The 911 seems to have given birth to an entire industry of aftermarket builders. DP Motorsports have gained a reputation for quality workmanship. 3 **1985 PORSCHE 928** This engine was new for '85, with an increase in displacement to 302ci and a 10 to 1 compression ratio. 4 **1982 PORSCHE 924 TURBO** 1982 marked the end of the 924 which had been given a turbo to increase performance. 5 **1982 PORSCHE 911SC** When the 944 was introduced in 1981 it was supposed to signal, yet again, the end of the line for the 911. But, as we all know, the 911 is harder to kill than Jason was in *Halloween* 1,2,3,4,5... 6 **1982 PORSCHE 924 TURBO** Conceptually, the 924 was the same car that Porsche sold to VW for its proposed sports car. When VW decided not to go ahead, Porsche bought back the design and released it as the 924. 7 **1984 PORSCHE 928** This is the longest and widest Porsche ever built.
OVERLEAF: 1987 911 TURBO SPORT

2, 3, 4 & 5 1987 PORSCHE 911 TURBO SPORT In addition to its solid performance figures, the Turbo Sport is also quite luxurious. The interior features such creature comforts as air conditioning, electric windows, AM/FM stereo cassette, 12-way power seats and, of course, leather trim. This model is twenty three years on from the original 911 and has all of 250% of the original horsepower. Only improved suspension and tyre technology has enabled the handling of this sports car to keep pace with its massively increased power output. It remains, however, a rather tricky car for those not used to powerful engines. **6 SPORTS PERFORMANCE CONVERSION PORSCHE** This is another striking example of an aftermarket Porsche conversion.

5

6

1987 PORSCHE 944 TURBO "Outstanding road manners"..."Best thing to happen to Porsche"..."Most innovative engineering." These were some of the comments made about his half-brother to the 928. Half-brother because its in line 4 powerplant ws simply the right half of the 928's V-8. The sohc turbocharged engine delivers 217hp, gets to 60mph in 6.1 seconds and tops out at 152 mph. Announced in 1985, the 944 Turbo scores over the ordinary 944 (if such a car can be called 'ordinary') by reducing the 0 to 60mph time from 8.4 seconds to 6.3 seconds and boosting the top speed from 137mph to 152mph, all achieved by adding a water cooled turbocharger to the engine resulting 220hp beneath the seemingly inane exterior. **OVERLEAF: 1987 PORSCHE 944 TURBO.**

2

3

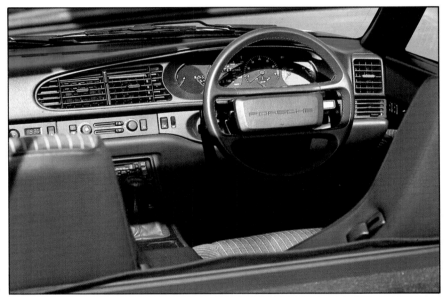

4

5

1988 PORSCHE 911 CARRERA CABRIO The Porsche 911 has been with us for a very long time, and if the Carrera Cabriolet is any indication, it will be around a while longer. Grand touring in the true sense of the term: comfortable, efficient, highspeed transport for two. Such magnificent performance is perhaps rather surprising considering the layout of the car. Unlike the majority of cars, the engine is placed at the rear of the car, behind the gearbox and the rear axle line. This might be expected to give poor handling with a tendency for rear-end slide, but Porsche engineering has managed to obviate the problem and create fine handling on even the powerful 911 Carrera Cabriolet.

2

3

4

5

1, 3, 5 & 6 1988 PORSCHE 959 The 959 may not look as exciting as the Ferrari F 40 or Lamborghini Countach, but this may be the supercar to beat all supercars. Fulltime, computer-controlled four-wheel drive is one reason. When cornering, the computer allocates power to whichever end of the car needs the most traction. Its twin-turbo dohc 450hp engine drives the 3220 lb. car from 0 to 60 in 3.9 seconds, with a top speed of 190mph.

2 & 4 1987 PORSCHE 928S 4 In 1987 the 928 became the 928S 4. To go with the name, a reengineered 5-litre, 316hp V-8 which, along with improved aerodynamics, pushed the car to 165mph.

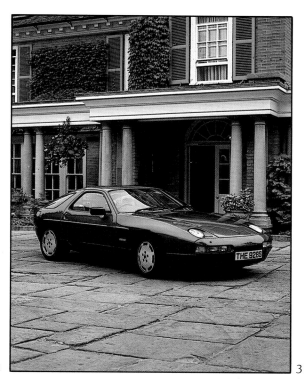

2

3

4

5

6

1 1989 PORSCHE 928S 4 For 1989 the luxurious 928S 4 is essentially unchanged. For most people that would seem to be enough. **2 & 4 1989 PORSCHE 944** In 1989 the front-engined, water-cooled 944 offered a larger 2681cc, 162hp engine that boosted performance and upped top speed to 137mph. **3 1987 GEMBALLA AVALANCHE PORSCHE** The Gemballa Avalanche was the hit of the 1985 Geneva Auto Show. Uwe Gemballa's company is in the Ruf, AMG league of top aftermarket builders. As he says in his brochure: "No wish, and particularly no special wish in connection with individualized production remains unfulfilled..." **5 1989 PORSCHE 944 TURBO** For '89 the 944 Turbo's performance was uprated with a 247hp, intercooled turbo engine that delivers 162mph top speed, ABS and a limited slip differential. **6 1989 PORSCHE 911** Fifty years from now, when gasoline powered cars are a thing of the past, there probably will be a new 911S (S for Solar). **OVERLEAF: 1989 PORSCHE 928S**

3

4

5

6

1

2

3

4

5

6

1 1911 RENAULT AX About this time the firm began to concentrate on the manufacture of road, rather than race, cars of which this two-seat runabout is a good example. **2 1934 RENAULT CELTAQUARTRE** Renault certainly knew how to name their cars in the 'twenties and 'thirties: Vivasix, Vivastella, Nervastella, Monaquartres, Vivaquartres, and in 1934, the Celtaquartre sedan. **3 1937 RENAULT CELTAQUARTRE** A convertible version of the popular Celtaquartre. **4 1962 RENAULT FLORIDE** The front-wheel-drive Floride appeared in 1962.. **5 1958 RENAULT 4 CV** The 4V was one of the most popular postwar European cars. One million were produced in ten years. **6 1988 RENAULT 5 GT TURBO** A mid-engine 1397cc intercooled turbo engine will take you from 0 to 60 in 8 seconds, and to a top speed of 125mph. **7 1988 RENAULT GTA TURBO** This futuristic design employs a composite body bonded to a steel-backbone chassis. **8 1970 RENAULT ALPINE A110** Jean Reédélé modified Renaults for use in the European Rally Championship. In 1955 he established the Alpine marque, which has now been absorbed into the Renault group.

1 **1934 RILEY IMP** The Imp's 4-cyl. powerplant was developed in 1927 for the Riley Nine and remained in use until 1957. 2 **1953 RILEY RMF** The 2.5-litre RMF was introduced in 1953 and remained in production until 1957. 3 **1937 RILEY SPRITE** The Sprite was the last of the classic Riley sports cars. The company, on the brink of financial disaster in 1938, was bought by Lord Nuffield who stated that he was "desirous of preserving in every way the development of those characteristics that have made the Riley car so outstanding." He didn't. 4 **1937 ROVER 10** Rover in the 'thirties was known for producing quality cars with economy in mind. With a view toward manufacturing efficiency, the model 10's, 12's, and 14's shared identical bodies while the 4-cyl. 1388cc 10's and 1496cc 12's shared the same chassis. 5 **1930 RUXTON** Front-wheel drive and a unique split gearbox allowed the Ruxton to be ten inches lower than its contemporaries. This "genuine lowness, ingeniously obtained" wasn't enough. After only two years in production, with fewer than 300 cars on the road, the Ruxton was history.

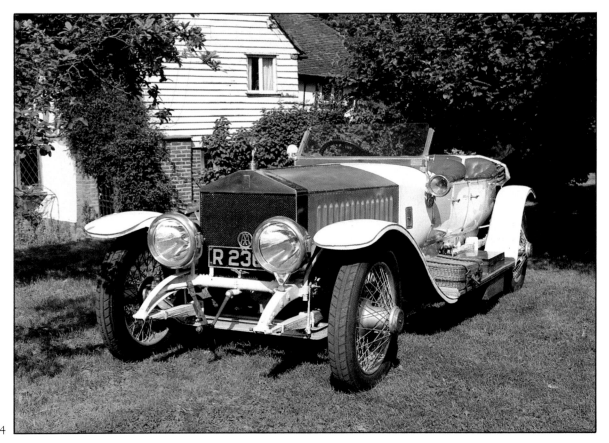

1 **1907 ROLLS-ROYCE SILVER GHOST** In April 1907, the thirteenth 40/50 chassis was made and it would become one of the most famous Rolls of all time. The body was painted silver with sliver plated fittings and a silver-plaque bearing its name: The Silver Ghost. 2, 3, 5 & 6 **ROLLS-ROYCE SILVER GHOST** Production of the Silver Ghost began in September 1907 with four chassis per week leaving the factory. The car was so successful that on March 2, 1908, the decision was made to produce no other types. This was quite a departure from what was considered the norm at the time, when a wide variety of of models was deemed necessary for success. The examples here: (**3**) a 1909, (**2**) a 1912 with Barker coachwork, (**5**) a 1914 model and (**6**) a boattail from the same year. 4 **1914 ROLLS-ROYCE ALPINE EAGLE** The Austrian Alpine Trials were held annually from 1910 to 1914. Silver Ghosts were prepared for 1913 featuring 4-speed gearboxes, and 70hp engines. They won, and soon replicas of the team cars were being marketed under the name Continental, although to many they would always be known as the Alpine Eagles.

1

1 1909 ROLLS-ROYCE SILVER GHOST Two major design changes occurred in the Silver Ghost series for 1909: engine size was increased from 7036cc to 7428cc, upping horsepower from 48 to 60, and the 4-speed gearbox was replaced by a 3-speed. 2 1911 ROLLS-ROYCE SILVER GHOST 1911 was the first year for the now famous mascot, the flying lady. 3 1911 ROLLS-ROYCE 40/50 SILVER GHOST Coachwork for the Silver Ghost was done by a number of firms. 4 1904 ROCHET-SCHNEIDER Rochet-Schneider ("The World's Greatest Hillclimbers") built in Lyon, France, from 1894 to 1932 offered unique metal-to- metal brakes that were cooled by a jet of water controlled by the driver. 5 1914 ROLLS-ROYCE ALPINE EAGLE

2

3

1 1929 ROLLS-ROYCE PHANTOM II In September 1929 the "New Phantom" (or Phantom I) was replaced by the Phantom II. The major changes were in the chassis. **2 1926 ROLLS- ROYCE PHANTOM I TOURER** The New Phantom was, in effect, an interim model between the venerable Silver Ghost and the more modern Phantom II. **3 1924 ROLLS- ROYCE SILVER GHOST LIMOUSINE** Another version of the long-lived Silver Ghost. **4 1929 ROLLS-ROYCE PHANTOM I** In 1928 the Phantom got a new aluminium cylinder head and probably developed 90hp in its original form and over 100hp in its final year of 1929. **5 1925 ROLLS-ROYCE TWENTY** The Twenty was one of the most popular of all Rolls models and its engine was to prove itself in various forms until 1959. **6 1925 ROLLS-ROYCE SPRINGFIELD SILVER GHOST STRATFORD CONVERTIBLE** Between 1919 and 1925 a number of Silver Ghosts were produced in the U.S. in Springfield, Mass.

1

2

3

4

5

1 & 2 ROLLS-ROYCE PHANTOM III This 1938 Phantom III had a 7341cc V-12 and magnificent coachwork by Hooper. **2** The '39 Sports Limousine featured independent front suspension, a 165hp V-12 and could hit 60 in 16 seconds. **3 1926 ROLLS-ROYCE PHANTOM TOURER** This example features coachwork by Barker. **4 1949 ROLLS-ROYCE SILVER WRAITH LIMOUSINE** The Silver Wraith was introduced in 1946. With the exception of limousines, like this example by Hooper, the standard wheelbase was 127 inches. **5 1930 ROLLS-ROYCE PHANTOM I** This Phantom features coachwork by the American firm of Brewster & Co. **6 1934 ROLLS-ROYCE PHANTOM II** The Phantom II, which was made from 1929 to 1935, is considered by many to be the most attractive Rolls-Royce ever produced.

1

2

3

4

1, 3 & 5 ROLLS-ROYCE PHANTOM II Available with either a 144- or 150-in. wheelbase, the Phantom II was a favourite of many coachbuilders. This 1930 short wheelbase All Weather Tourer (1) features coachwork by T.H. Gill, the 1931 version (3) by Brewster & Co. of New York and the 1934 Drophead Coupe (177-5) by H.J. Mulliner. **2 1939 ROLLS-ROYCE WRAITH** Some Rolls-Royce enthusiasts of the time thought the Wraith to be inferior to its predecessor, the 25/30. One published comment described the Wraith as a "slightly pregnant 25/30." The Wraith did offer customers a new welded chassis and independent front suspension. **4 1932 ROLLS-ROYCE 20/25 TORPEDO** The 20/25 had a 3669cc, 70hp engine that moved the cars along at about 75mph. The 20/25 laid the groundwork the first postwar models.

1

2

3

4

1 1976 ROLLS-ROYCE SILVER SHADOW MK 1
Introduced in 1965, more than 2,000 modifications were made to the model before 1977. **2 1978 ROLLS-ROYCE CORNICHE CONVERTIBLE** In 1967 a Silver Shadow convertible was made by Mulliner Park Ward and in 1971 this model became the Corniche. **3 1985 ROLLS-ROYCE SILVER SPUR LIMOUSINE** This stretch limousine by B. Jankel was built by adding 42 inches to the long wheelbase version of the Silver Spur Sedan. **4 1963 ROLLS-ROYCE PHANTOM V** The Phantom V was the largest standard Rolls ever built. **5 1978 ROLLS-ROYCE CAMARGUE** The Camargue body was designed by Pininfarina and made its debut in 1973. It reached the end of its 531-car production run in 1986. **6 1974 ROLLS-ROYCE PHANTOM VI** Introduced in 1968, the Phantom VI was similar to its predecessor, the V, in all but detail changes. It was produced in small numbers until 1983.

1987 ROLLS-ROYCE SILVER SPIRIT This is the current standard Rolls-Royce and, like their previous models, it is far from standard, at least by anyone else's standards. Powered by a 6.7 litre V-8 with four-wheel independent suspension and the usual (for Rolls-Royce) burled walnut trim and Connolloy hide upholstery, make this the dream transportation of choice for aspiring moguls. Though when first introduced this model came in for a certain degree of criticism in Britain for its square headlight layout and rather 'American' rear, it has since become established as a true 'Roller.' One of the most ingenious features was the retractable mascot. If touched, the mascot promptly sinks into the radiator to be safe from the hands of would-be mascot collectors. As with all cars of this marque the engineering of the powerplant and transmission are equal to the quality of the luxurious finishing, ensuring smooth, quiet and largely trouble-free motoring for those fortunate enough to own these premier saloons.

1

2

3

4

5

1 1931 SINGER The Singer Company trailed only Morris and Austin among English automakers in 1931. A wide variety of models were offered, including the Tourer and this Junior Tourer which got around on only 10hp. **2 1933 SINGER LE MANS** Designed by A.G. Booth, the Sports Nine finished 13th at Le Mans in 1933, prompting Singer to dub this model the "Le Mans." **3 1914 STAR** This 4-cyl., 3016cc 15.9hp model, introduced in 1912, is the most famous of all the types produced by the Star Engineering Co. An early victim of the Depression, Star suspended production in 1932. **5 1909 SHEFFIELD-SIMPLEX TYPE AC 2** Designed by Percy Richardson, this model featured a 6-cyl., 45hp bi-block engine and two-pedal control. It was available in a "gearboxless" version (for "shiftless" drivers, no doubt).

1 1978 ROLLS-ROYCE CAMARGUE In 1978 the Camargue was the most expensive Rolls-Royce offered. **2 1961 ROLLS-ROYCE SILVER CLOUD II** The Silver Cloud II was introduced with a new 6230cc V-8 and, for the first time, standard automatic transmission. **3 1959 ROLLS-ROYCE SILVER CLOUD** The Silver CLoud first appeared in 1955 and had the 4887cc engine found in the '54 Bentley Continental. **4 1963 ROLLS-ROYCE SILVER CLOUD III** This final development of the Silver Cloud came in 1962. It had a higher compression ratio, which boosted power by approximately 8 percent. **5 1963 ROLLS-ROYCE PHANTOM V** At the time of the V-8's introduction in the Silver Cloud II, Rolls-Royce announced a new chassis expressly for limousine coachwork: the Phantom V.

1 1976 ROLLS-ROYCE SILVER SHADOW MK 1
Introduced in 1965, more than 2,000 modifications were made to the model before 1977. **2 1978 ROLLS-ROYCE CORNICHE CONVERTIBLE** In 1967 a Silver Shadow convertible was made by Mulliner Park Ward and in 1971 this model became the Corniche. **3 1985 ROLLS-ROYCE SILVER SPUR LIMOUSINE** This stretch limousine by B. Jankel was built by adding 42 inches to the long wheelbase version of the Silver Spur Sedan. **4 1963 ROLLS-ROYCE PHANTOM V** The Phantom V was the largest standard Rolls ever built. **5 1978 ROLLS-ROYCE CAMARGUE** The Camargue body was designed by Pininfarina and made its debut in 1973. It reached the end of its 531-car production run in 1986. **6 1974 ROLLS-ROYCE PHANTOM VI** Introduced in 1968, the Phantom VI was similar to its predecessor, the V, in all but detail changes. It was produced in small numbers until 1983.

1987 ROLLS-ROYCE SILVER SPIRIT This is the current standard Rolls-Royce and, like their previous models, it is far from standard, at least by anyone else's standards. Powered by a 6.7 litre V-8 with four-wheel independent suspension and the usual (for Rolls-Royce) burled walnut trim and Connolloy hide upholstery, make this the dream transportation of choice for aspiring moguls. Though when first introduced this model came in for a certain degree of criticism in Britain for its square headlight layout and rather 'American' rear, it has since become established as a true 'Roller' One of the most ingenious features was the retractable mascot. If touched, the mascot promptly sinks into the radiator to be safe from the hands of would-be mascot collectors. As with all cars of this marque the engineering of the powerplant and transmission are equal to the quality of the luxurious finishing, ensuring smooth, quiet and largely trouble-free motoring for those fortunate enough to own these premier saloons.

1 **1931 SINGER** The Singer Company trailed only Morris and Austin among English automakers in 1931. A wide variety of models were offered, including the Tourer and this Junior Tourer which got around on only 10hp. 2 **1933 SINGER LE MANS** Designed by A.G. Booth, the Sports Nine finished 13th at Le Mans in 1933, prompting Singer to dub this model the "Le Mans." 3 **1914 STAR** This 4-cyl., 3016cc 15.9hp model, introduced in 1912, is the most famous of all the types produced by the Star Engineering Co. An early victim of the Depression, Star suspended production in 1932. 5 **1909 SHEFFIELD-SIMPLEX TYPE AC 2** Designed by Percy Richardson, this model featured a 6-cyl., 45hp bi-block engine and two-pedal control. It was available in a "gearboxless" version (for "shiftless" drivers, no doubt).

6

7

6 - 9 STUDEBAKER Studebaker began operations as a manufacturer of wagons in 1854. They began automotive production in 1904 and by the 1930's were established as one of America's top ten automakers. The 1931 President convertible (**8**) was powered by a straight 8. This model and the 45 Limousine (**6**) were dropped in favor of smaller sixes when the company went into receivership in 1933. Under new management, the company resumed production, and by the early 'fifties had regained their place as one of the top independents. The 1954 Commander V-8 (**7**) was designed under the supervision of Raymond Loewy. The 4244cc, 200hp V-8 1956 Sky Hawk (**9**) was also a product of the Loewy studios, and was one of the most effective designs of the period.

8

9

1 1931 SUNBEAM 16 SALOON Noted for smoothness, ease of handling and careful engineering, the Sunbeams of the period had many racing successes, including the first Grand Prix victory by a British marque in the 1923 French GP. The 16, introduced in 1927, had a 2-litre, 44hp straight 6. **2, 3 & 6 TALBOT LAGO** Introduced by Anthony Lago in 1947, the T-26 Grand Sport (**2 & 3**) featured a 190hp 4.5-litre engine that could move the gorgeous Saouchik-bodied car to 125mph. The earlier T 150 SS Coupe of 1939 (**3**) had coachwork by Figoni et Falaschi. **4 & 5 STUTZ** The 1929 Stutz Model M 322ci straight 8 (**4**) was the last model produced before the new SV-16 and DV-32 went on the market. The 1933 DV-32 featured a 156hp dohc 32- valve engine and came with a factory guarantee that each DV-32 had been tested in excess of 100mph prior to shipment from the factory. It was true, but the truth wasn't enough, and in 1937 Stutz folded.

1

2

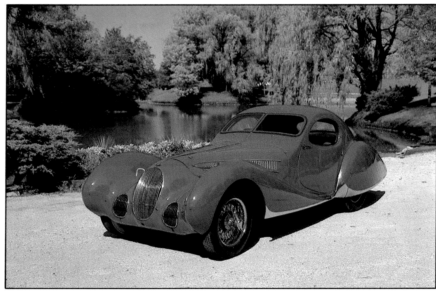

3

4